Growing Forward is a sensible and caring companion through difficult phases of life change. It reinforces that change isn't about toughness and willpower, but about harnessing our unique individual qualities inside of us. The book harnesses the best of positive psychology in a practical guide to bringing about personal transformation and improving our lives.

Dr Elliot Wilson, Psychiatrist and Therapist

Growing Forward is an easy to read, practical handbook on how to deal with, understand and improve life's challenges and apparent setbacks.

I love the "plane speak" and plain speak for it's no-nonsense approach to dealing with life and the curve balls that come with it.

My favourite is Chapter 8, TAKE ACTION – FROM A DIFFERENT PERSPECTIVE, for its pragmatic approach to acknowledging your strengths, weaknesses, and key attributes. The exercises are practical and "do-able" and the real-life examples Charlotte uses give insight into her career as a pilot. Charlotte has a gift for writing it as raw and real as it gets.

A great read which I highly recommend to anyone wanting to take charge of their thoughts and emotions, and to better understand themselves to become their greatest potential."

Michelle Huntington,
Airline Captain, Keynote Speaker,
Leadership Coach, Podcast Host

Charlotte has reminded me that we are human beings first, and human doings second. Great personal stories, techniques and tools to help you strengthen your foundations to cope with and embrace inevitable change in life.

Dylan Lennox, Management Consultant

My personal mission in life is to live to my fullest potential and hopefully lead by example by not allowing myself to be held back by anything or anyone (even if that is my own self-doubt!). *Growing Forward* so closely aligns to this mission and reconfirms a lot of my personal views and ways of approaching the world. As you would expect from an airline pilot, Charlotte's approach is clear, well-structured and logical. It provides a practical path to living to your values, questioning your impact on the world and being all that you can be. It is easy to read, and the exercises are simple yet thought provoking. You will get to the end of the book without realising the transformation that you have just experienced. It is a practical step by step guide that takes the pressure off the big questions and will leave you grateful and ready for your next step. Enjoy!

Min Swan,
President, Sunshine Coast Business Women's Network

Reading *Growing Forward* feels like having a personal conversation with the author. The style is warm and approachable and the book provides new insights and perspectives which reach a level of depth that stays with me. I have been inspired by the author's emphasis on the importance of valuing our own strengths and abilities. This perspective is something I will carry forward in my own leadership. The reminder that significant change can be achieved through small steps is powerful and relevant.

Ulrika Sigerud, Judge

Wow, what a book. I work with neuro-leadership, leadership development and behaviour change, and can say; this book is very helpful. In plain language, it deals with a big subject where people often meet resistance.

Many think about changing things in their environment/business, but few think about changing themselves.

The author delivers practical and easy ways to really bring about change. Her own personal stories make everything in the book feel genuine and plausible. It encourages the reader to take on the exercises and their own situation. The book makes me pause and reflect. It all starts with me. I can only take responsibility for my own life and self-leadership. I am reminded of my own promise to never let my fears rule my life but to change what I need in order to live at my full capacity.

I warmly recommend this book to anyone who wants to find the best version of themselves.

Johanna Gittne,
Leadership Developer, Behavioural Scientist and Author.

We all face adversities and challenges in life, but how we respond to them will determine how well or not we get through them. Charlotte uses concepts from psychology and neuroscience, as well as her own experience, to illustrate how we can be our best selves with meaningful lives, even in the face of adversity. She does this in a way that is easy to understand and apply practically. *Growing Forward* is a well written book, which, if what Charlotte suggests is put into practice, has the potential to transform your life.

Carol Stewart,
Executive Coach, 5 x LinkedIn Top Voice UK,
and Author of *Quietly Visible*

There is much value and insight to be gained from reading this book. What I loved most about *Growing Forward* is the way Charlotte Hillenbrand gently guides you as the gifted coach she is, it is like having a close friend explain how to transform with ease. Charlotte takes you on a journey of self-discovery from the comfortable seat of being yourself. You will be enlightened by how owning all parts of you; your strengths and the parts you want to hide, enables you to grow forward from a place of empowerment. You will be encouraged to take small steps, dispelling any feelings of overwhelm and be provided tools to coax yourself forward.

The book is structured and progresses logically and easily from one section to the next. Charlotte generously shares her own experience in using the explained techniques providing helpful reference, insight and trust. Following years of reading self-help books, from *Growing Forward* I finally received the guidance and ability to change, and I did!

Karina

Growing Forward is a fabulous book! With a very friendly and approachable feel to it, it is relatable, easy to consume and filled with practical ideas and exercises that are at once effective and very doable. What a wonderful resource for anyone looking for a roadmap for their "what's next" chapter.

Trisha Bright,
Executive Coach, Happiness & Emotional Intelligence Expert

I love the way this book breaks down the process of change using Charlotte's own experience of transitioning from a career as a pilot to becoming a coach. Charlotte's approach to communicating the complexities of neuroscience and positive psychology in relation to people's ability to change is totally refreshing. I'm really grateful to have this book to dip into if I need motivation, inspiration and practical advice at any stage in my journey, especially as I am going through massive positive change for myself and my business.

Jane Turner, Author Coach and Publishing Strategist

Life is a series of changes – and this book may be just the thing you need to learn how to navigate through those changes. And what better way to learn how to navigate than from a former pilot! Charlotte shares her experiences and expertise on how to find the best version of you and become more resilient to overcome any change. Who wouldn't want that? Worth a read!

Lizzie Korsgaard, Career Coach

Read this book!

Change is happening around us all the time. Charlotte shares generously from her story and gives us powerful yet simple tools to tackle this change from within. She shows us practical ways to take control of our thoughts so that we may determine our direction of travel and become the master of our own journey.

Christer Andersson, Founder of the ID Group, Serial entrepreneur

In this book, Charlotte beautifully takes the reader on a journey of self-reflection, self-discovery and self-appreciation. At the same time the book is sprinkled with very interesting, fascinating and insightful examples and stories of Charlotte's personal life, her career as a pilot and life-changing circumstances.

What truly stood out to me when reading this book was Charlotte's gentle approach of nudging the reader to embrace change and be resourceful. The simple yet impactful exercises in this book help the reader realise that they have everything they need within them to create the life they long for.

Having gone through a big transition myself in my personal and professional life recently, I enjoyed reading this book and reflecting on the exercises in each chapter.

Charlotte manages to evoke a mindset of ease and a genuine appreciation for the opportunities that come with change.

Anne Koopmann-Schmidt,
Leadership Coach and Team Development Consultant

ABOUT THE AUTHOR

Charlotte Hillenbrand is the lawyer who became an international airline pilot and then an author, speaker, mentor and coach. She is passionate about human potential, and advocates everyone's power to be their own agent for change.

Her expertise in the field of change comes from personal experience and study. A complete career pivot after 15+ years as an international airline pilot forced Charlotte to consolidate her skills and experiences that took her from the courts to the cockpit of a widebody jet and then out from it with her optimism intact. She combined this with her interest in applied neuroscience and positive psychology to develop a framework that helps people navigate change with ease.

Charlotte writes and speaks about the fact that every individual can access agency and resilience, and shows her readers simple and efficient ways to do that.

Charlotte grew up in Sweden, has studied at universities in Sweden, USA and France, as well as lived and worked in Germany and Switzerland before settling with her husband and their two daughters on the Sunshine Coast in Australia.

www.charlottehillenbrand.com.au
ch@charlottehillenbrand.com.au

GROWING *Forward*

NAVIGATING CHANGE WITH EASE

CHARLOTTE HILLENBRAND

Published by the Power Writers Publishing Group in 2023.

Copyright © 2023 Charlotte Hillenbrand

All Rights Reserved. No part of this book may be reproduced by any mechanical, photographic, or electronic processes, or in the form of a phonographic recording. Nor may be stored in a retrieval system, transmitted or otherwise be copied for public or private use other than for 'fair use' – as brief quotations embodied in articles and reviews, without prior written permission of the author.

ISBN:978-0-6456271-4-5

A catalogue record for this book is available from the National Library of Australia

Cover design by Miriam Rudolph.

Internal layout by Andrew Davies.

Project Management by Jane Turner.

Disclaimer

Any opinions expressed in this work are exclusively those of the author and are not necessarily the views held or endorsed by others quoted throughout. All of the information, exercises and concepts contained within the publication are intended for general information only. The author does not take any responsibility for any choices that any individual or organization may make relating to this information in the business, personal, financial, familial or other areas of life. If any individual or organization does wish to implement the ideas discussed herein, it is recommended that they obtain their own independent advice specific to their circumstances.

DEDICATION

For my husband Patrick who is always my rock.

For my daughters Nellie and Mia
who constantly inspire me
and have taught me so much,
not least from the way they handled change themselves
during the years of transition that the whole family
has been through.

"You have brains in your head.

You have feet in your shoes.

You can steer yourself

Any direction you choose."

– Dr. Seuss

CONTENTS

FOREWORD	17
PREFACE	19
INTRODUCTION	22

PART 1: PRE-DEPARTURE
Assessing all you already have — 31
- Chapter 1: Strengths — 33
- Chapter 2: Mindset — 47
- Chapter 3: A Head Full of Thoughts — 53
- Chapter 4: Embrace the Rest of You — 81

PART 2: DESIRED DESTINATION
Getting clarity around where you want to go — 87
- Chapter 5: Values — 89
- Chapter 6: A Few Thoughts on Purpose — 107
- Chapter 7: Goals — 111

PART 3: TAKE OFF
Doing things differently — 119
- Chapter 8: Take Action – from a Different Perspective — 121
- Chapter 9: Your Mind Can Hold You Back — 149
- Chapter 10: Coax Yourself Forward — 155

CONCLUSION	165
END NOTE	167

FOREWORD

I never flew on a flight with Charlotte as the pilot, but I can imagine what that was like. Her calm, measured, and highly competent demeanour would have ensured a comfortable and safe ride. So too, her book, *Growing Forward* provides readers with a smooth, gentle, and well-considered invitation to embark on a journey of self-discovery.

In this book you will find wisdom, attained from Charlotte's own journey of self-reflection, together with neuroscientific and psychological concepts, distilled into relevant, accessible, and easy to apply examples. Rather than ploughing through a maze of heavy scientific jargon and explanations of neuronal plasticity as evidenced by functional magnetic resonance imaging, you can imagine yourself walking through a meadow, creating a path to a chosen destination.

This book provides a plethora of simple, actionable steps that will assist those who are on a quest to find their "transferable you", but also those who simply want to do life better. Raising your awareness of your strengths and desires, as well as your values and your possibilities, can only enhance your life – even if it is already heading roughly in the direction you think you want to go. Giving yourself the opportunity to explore from the inside out holds the intriguing possibility of finding more. I encourage you to give yourself that gift.

As you journey through this book, you will have the opportunity to reflect, re-evaluate and reconsider your thoughts, feelings, and behaviours. Just like an audit of your finances, this personal audit will empower you to chart a new direction (if that is what you decide), or more fully appreciate the direction you are already taking.

You may be challenged, even confronted, by some of the content, particularly when you discover that, in the words of a popular song, you are indeed the problem. However, you will also be empowered and energised when you discover that, equally, you are the solution.

Regardless of your reason for reading this book, congratulate yourself, because you have made a good choice. It will take you on a journey, and the co-captain at the helm is trustworthy, wise, and, most importantly, well equipped to guide and support you, as *you* take the controls.

Enjoy the journey. The destination, whatever you decide it to be, will be worth it.

Kate Witteveen, PhD
Author, Coach and Mental Health Academic
Brisbane, February 2023

PREFACE

I had just been told that the damage to my eye was such that it no longer fulfilled the requirements for a pilot. Over the weeks and months to come it would become clear that the damage was irreversible and irreparable.

I had just lost my career.

It had been 18 months since I did my last flight as an airline pilot, from Hong Kong to Melbourne in the Airbus 330 I had been flying for the last few years.

Since that flight, along with most of my colleagues, I had been dealing with the effects of the Covid-19 pandemic. The world had closed down, and the aviation industry had just about disappeared overnight. For me, it meant that I lost my job as an airline pilot.

I managed to remain positive then. In my mind, I saw myself on a hiatus from flying for a couple of years or so before the industry would turn back up and I could return to the cockpit. I figured this was an opportunity to do something different, learn some new things, and enjoy family time at home after having lived half of my life in hotel rooms. In fact, I felt like I was making up for lost time and I was revelling in learning and exploring different sides of myself.

I found myself contemplating topics around strength, confidence, and resilience. I wondered what was keeping me so positive even after losing the job that I loved and had worked so hard to get. Among other things, I was curious about where my strength and resilience came from, and I made a point of having conversations with other professional women about what they regarded as strength and confidence in others and themselves. I noticed some definite patterns emerging, and I started to formulate my thoughts, without knowing that my interest in these things was going to turn into a passion, which would later turn into this book.

That's when my eye 'broke'. A chronic infection of my eye, which had been kept at bay for several years, got out of hand and took much of the vision from my left eye.

It was very clear to me right away that losing my job was nothing, compared to losing my ability to do the job. To make matters worse, the airline industry had started rehiring pilots and I knew that I would soon have been back up in the air. I felt like I had been dumped by a wave, lost my footing and my bearings, and didn't know what was up and what was down. I was frightened, lost and confused.

This was when push came to shove: It was a case of sink or swim. I had to ask myself the tough questions like – Who am I now? Will the kind of strength and resilience I'd been investigating be able to hold up under this kind of pressure? And most importantly, how was I going to get myself to higher ground so I could go on living a life that was just as interesting as the life I lived as an airline pilot?

What I did was leverage everything I've learnt through my life so far, and draw on all the strength I could muster.

This book is my outstretched hand to anyone who feels like they've lost their bearings for one reason or other. I have written this book because we all need to navigate our way through uncertainty and change from time to time, and I'm hoping it helps you to know that you are not alone and that you can learn from me.

The thing is that sometimes change is forced upon us like it was for me, and other times we're more on the front foot and get to initiate it ourselves. Maybe we realise we've outgrown a situation or reached a point where we have spare capacity that we want to put to good use. Have you ever had that feeling that you're not sure what you want to change, but you just feel like something needs to change?

Whichever category you fall into, I believe you will gain a deeper sense of clarity and momentum as you develop a new way of looking at yourself and your untapped potential. I will even go so far as to say that if you read this book in a deliberate way, it has the power to change your life!

I smile as I think about the fact that there's no way I would have made such an audacious statement before going through what I've been through over the last couple of years. My hope is that this book will help you transform the trajectory of your life by tapping into the incredible resources we all have inside but usually don't find until the going gets really tough. With any luck, you've found this book before getting to that point.

INTRODUCTION

This book is about navigating change.

I believe the best way to do that is by finding the best version of you. When you are the best version of you, you are resilient and confident. When you are the best version of you, it doesn't matter what goes on around you, as you are able to adapt to many different tasks, settings and circumstances. The best version of you can fit in anywhere you want or need to be.

When you are the best version of you, you are

- Working to your strengths.
  Your strengths are not just skills that come naturally to you and you have developed over time, but also the way you behave, think and do things.
- Guided by your values, consciously and actively using them as your compass when you make choices and decisions.
- Turning up as all that you are, not just the good parts.
  That's right; to be the best version of you, you also need to accept the worst parts of you.
- Aware of the thoughts in your head, so you can choose thoughts that are helpful to you.
- Taking responsibility for your own actions and inactions, as that is the most powerful way to be.
- Able to look for and see different perspectives in order to find solutions.
- Not afraid of failing as you know it is a natural and harmless part of learning.

It is the version of you that is most equipped to face change. Ironically, when you shift into the best version of you, you may find that you don't even need any further change. Finding the best version of you will give you clarity, confidence, and fulfilment.

That's what I found when I had to pick myself up and build a new life. When I lost my job people talked to me about transferable skills. That's all well and good, but I found that it wasn't enough; I wanted to find a transferable me. I wasn't looking so much for what I could do, but for who I was. And when I found that, the doing came naturally.

For years I had been interested in the brain and our thoughts. I had read books about neuroplasticity and positive psychology. When I now found myself with a future I had to reshape, I related what I was reading to my own experiences. I was particularly interested in getting to the bottom of what traits had taken me into the cockpit of a widebody jet, and now out of it with my optimism intact.

In what I came to think of as my hiatus project, I formed some surprising conclusions about what strength can look like, which lead to my thinking about how we can leverage it to make change easier. I also reflected on the fact that a common reaction I got when people found out that I was a pilot, was "Wow!" I guess that wow was an expression of admiration for something they deemed impressive. I was never comfortable with that reaction, for a number of reasons: I have never felt like a wow kind of person; I never knew what my response to that was supposed to be; I didn't know how to deflect the wow without at the same time depreciating myself (which I saw no reason to do), and I didn't know how to deflect the wow without somehow also depreciating the other person by invalidating their reaction.

But most of all it was because of this: We all have so many impressive strengths inside of us.

What you need to do is find *your* strengths, and find out what makes *you* tick. This is where you'll find the very best version of *you*. Everyone has a best version of themselves. That version is effortlessly strong, resilient, confident and happy.

All of these different aspects prompted me to write this book. I want to share what I leaned on when I had to navigate my way through so much change after the loss of my career. I am sharing what I have learned and experienced so that you can learn from me, recognise your strengths even if they don't look like what you expected them to, and be able to live your wow. I want you to know that small shifts in your perspective and the habits you have around your thought processes can have huge effects on the outcome, and through them, you can reshape the way you act and react in your life.

Living your wow will give you clarity, confidence, fulfilment, and resilience, that you will experience in your own unique way.

In this book, I will show you how finding the best version of you is the most effective way to navigate change.

Finding the best version of you is the most effective way to navigate change.

This is how we will do it.

First, we will look at all that you already have. I will help you see your strengths, your accomplishments, and your strongest traits so that you can get a good view of your own greatness. No matter what kind of shift you are wanting or needing to make, I dare say you have more to work with than you give yourself credit for. I say that because if you are like most people, some of your strengths will be in disguise. I will show you how to leverage everything

INTRODUCTION

you have at your disposal into the ability to change. You will also gain an understanding of why you might be resisting – resisting change itself, and resisting acknowledging your own greatness. There are explanations to be found both in neuroscience and psychology. It is not just you! It is not just a matter of willpower. Knowing this, I hope, will take some of the pressure off you. You will see that simply being aware of this inner resistance will help you make conscious choices, and you will find it easier to see that change and growth are not as difficult as you might have thought.

Next, we will look at your thoughts. We will talk about how the thoughts in your head are just that – thoughts. They don't necessarily represent the truth. You will learn how to become aware of your thoughts, especially habitual thoughts that tend to take the form of limiting beliefs. It is useful to take stock of your habitual thoughts so that you can keep the ones that help you and discard the ones that are not serving you well. This new awareness of your thoughts will enable you to choose more helpful ones whenever you need to. Awareness is essential for change to take place because you can only do something about things you are aware of.

After you have taken stock of all that you are, we will raise our eyes and look outwards. Introspection is necessary to create awareness, but the purpose of this awareness is to enable you to deliberately and authentically show up as the best version of yourself in your family, at your work and in your community. To this end, we will also be looking at your desired 'destination' so that you will gain clarity about what you can achieve. That's what Part 2 of this book is focussed on. We will do this, not by looking at actions and outcomes, but instead by looking at what drives you. By the end of Part 2, you will see how aligning your choices and decisions with your values will give you clarity, confidence and resilience.

This inside-out perspective might surprise you, but I'm sure you will see the benefits of it as you read along. There will likely be several things that feel counter-intuitive to you in this book. That is one of the reasons I'm writing it. When I pieced together my experiences, there were many instances where I found myself seeing things in a different light. That's what allowed the biggest breakthroughs to happen for me. I hope it will help you like that too.

Once you are more aware of what you are and what drives you, it is time to take action. With the groundwork you have already done it will seem easy for you to walk in the direction of your desired outcomes. You will be motivated from within, and you will see that the change you are creating is not dependent on any situation or set of circumstances. Rather, the change you are creating is allowing you to be your best self wherever you choose or need to be.

You'll also gain awareness of some things that can trip you up, as well as what you can do to get yourself moving in the right direction again.

By the time you get to the last chapter, you will have gained clarity about the change you want to see in yourself and your life, and how to bring it about. You will have removed a lot of resistance, and you will have gained the momentum you need to move forward with effortless ease.

Throughout the book, you will find exercises that will help you gain awareness and insights that will drive your change. I suggest that you do each exercise as it comes and write your notes on the empty pages provided at the end of each chapter. I myself used to skip similar exercises in books I read, telling myself I would get back to them later. Or I would read them, and briefly think about the answers in my head before I moved on. Then I learnt the very obvious, and therefore maybe too simple truth that no tool works unless you actually use it.

I started doing the exercises that someone I wanted to learn from suggested – and wouldn't you know it, it worked. That's why I suggest that like me, you change your habit and do the exercises as they come up. This matters because for you to be able to get anything from any of the tools at your disposal, you need to not only use it, but use it the way it was intended. There are empty pages for note-taking throughout this book, so you have no excuse!

Furthermore, taking notes rather than just thinking about the questions and your answers, is important because it will activate several different areas in your brain. This in turn will make a bigger imprint on your brain and increase your chances of remembering and retrieving the information when you need it. It also adds clarity to what you have been thinking about by way of a visual representation of your conscious and unconscious mind. So to make the most of the resource you are holding in your hand, grab a pen or pencil and do each exercise as it comes.

You might not know it yet, but you are stronger and more capable than you think. When you become aware of all your strengths and learn how to think helpful thoughts, you will be able to live your life more deliberately, with more confidence and purpose. That way you will be more fulfilled and resilient than you probably thought was possible.

Be advised that this book is not a scientific work. Although I sometimes refer to other experts' works, I do not quote scientifically or make any scientific claims of my own. I am not qualified to give advice or make suggestions to anyone who is suffering from mental ill health. Please know that it is a strength to look for help from a mental health professional when you need to.

Before we get into the book, on the next page I am prompting you to start with the end in mind. This is my way of helping you sense a powerful future belonging, so you can then use this book deliberately to create real change in your life.

Before you do anything, else I want you to do this:

I want you to imagine yourself on your 70th birthday. You are fit and healthy, with a great life behind you and lots of energy left to fill many more years. You are happy and content in the middle of a life well lived, and people have stopped by on your special day to congratulate you and all that you have achieved so far. Someone asks you "What is it like to be such a successful …?"

Finish that sentence. Close your eyes and imagine yourself in that scene on your big birthday, when someone asks you that question, and answer it for yourself. Try out a few different answers, then choose the one that lights you up the most.

Now, imagine that is what's on the other side of the transition ahead of you. Think of that person with joy and energy. This will be the fuel that drives you forward through your change. At this point, it is all you need in the way of a goal.

Whenever you feel confused or frustrated or disheartened during your change I want you to return to this image of a happy healthy successful 70-year-old you.

PART 1

PRE-DEPARTURE

Assessing all you already have

If you are reading this, I am guessing that you want or need to create a shift or a change of some sort in order to move forward in your life. Maybe change has been thrust upon you like it was for me. Or maybe you have decided you want change and are ready to get into it. Or maybe this is you: you are a high-performing, smart and driven person who has already achieved many things in your life and have nothing to complain about really. But still … still, there is *something* that needs to change. Like a small stone in your shoe, you have tried to ignore it; after all, you are getting by just fine the way things are. But each step is getting a bit more uncomfortable, almost to the point of being painful, and when you finally stop to get rid of that stone you wish you'd done it earlier so that you would have been able to walk on in comfort.

This, right now, is the moment when you stop and take the stone out of your shoe.

Whether you're in the 'nothing to complain about' camp, or the 'change has been thrust upon you' camp, the problem is the same: you need to find a new way forward. The solution is also the same. It's about knowing what you already have, and what you need, then finding a way to bridge the gap, and (importantly) going on to actually doing it. In saying this I don't want to trivialise the problem. Far from it, I know how lost and confused one can feel when faced with big changes. My hope is instead that when you see that there are just a few clear steps between you and the change you are seeking, you will realise that it is doable. This will take away some of the overwhelm you might be feeling around the prospect of change.

Throughout this book, I will help you bring some order to your current disorder. I will do this mainly by suggesting new perspectives that might be useful. With a fresh set of eyes, you might pick up things about yourself and your life that you haven't noticed before. You might find that instead of creating one specific change, you create a transformation with a ripple effect that shows up everywhere. Instead of finding your transferable skills, we are setting out to find the transferable you.

In short, in the first part of the book, you will assess all that you already have; all that you already are.

Chapter 1

STRENGTHS

Do you sometimes find yourself so engrossed in something that you seem to forget time and space? You are completely focused, your work feels effortless and joyful, solutions are found, and things fall into place. You are in a flow, and when you 'resurface' from this state you feel energised, not drained, even if you have just had a long productive work session. I hope you've had a chance to experience this state because working from our strengths energises us and leaves us feeling happy and fulfilled.

Research shows that when you get to work from your strengths everyone benefits. You are happy, fulfilled and more productive and have energy left over at the end of the day, your employer gets to enjoy the fruits of your labour, and those around you get to enjoy your increased energy and uplifted mood. Unfortunately, research also shows that only about 20 percent of us work from our strengths on a daily basis.

Historically, psychology used to be focused on helping people get from an unhealthy mental state to a healthy mental state, from minus to zero on a scale, if you will.

When the American Psychological Association inaugurated its new president Martin Seligman in 1996, he declared that psychologists also needed to study what makes people happy, fulfilled and more productive, rather than just fix what was 'wrong' with them. Thus, the discipline of positive psychology was formed. It studies what takes people from zero along the positive side of the scale; what makes life most worth living. Positive psychology recognises that developing our strengths is key to a good life. While working on developing our weak areas can be necessary in some instances, this can only constitute damage control and prevent failure. Real development, acceleration and progress happen when we work from and develop our strengths.

Yet our society is very deficit focused. We seem to think that evaluation is all about finding what went wrong so we don't repeat the same mistakes. What about evaluating what we did right and finding ways to incorporate more of that?

Of course, in certain cases it is essential to fix a deficiency of one kind or other, but more often than you might think, we can simply let go of what's bothering us instead. That will free us up to shift our time and focus onto something aligned with our strengths. This is a space where the potential to change is ripe.

What I'm getting at here is that I want you to shift your focus from what's wrong to what's strong. That is the fundamental shift this book is inviting you to make.

Shift your focus from what's wrong to what's strong.

There are many ways to look at strengths and assess what yours are. We will spend some time in the next few sections on different aspects of strength so that you will be able to define some of yours.

Strength doesn't always look the way we expect it to

I did my pilot training at an air force base in Sweden. My male classmates and I were learning to fly commercial planes, but the training was hosted and equipped by the air force. We lived on the base for the 16-month duration of the training. I was the only woman in the group. The guys and I spent all our time together; we went to class together, studied together, exercised together, and ate dinner together every night. We became close-knit as a group, and I felt well-accepted and included. However, over time a certain jargon developed in the group, as it often does when people live close together like that. A few months into our training that jargon had gotten ruder and cruder, and even though much of it was quite general, some of it was aimed at me as the only woman there. I hated the way this made me feel, and I got to the point where I had well and truly had enough of it. It was definitely not what I had signed up for! I knew I had earned my right to be there just as much as my male classmates had, and I knew they were much nicer guys than this. Not only had I had enough of their jargon, but I knew we could do better. So, I decided to talk to them about it.

One evening at the dinner table I plucked up enough courage to say something. Yes, it was a matter of plucking up my courage. My inner dialogue had almost talked me out of it, trying to tell me that it wasn't so bad, that I could surely suck it up and soldier on, but this time I decided it was something I *had* to do. Eventually, I managed to tell my classmates that it had gone too far and that I had had enough of it. I went on to make the point that even if I didn't expect or want special treatment, I had the right to be treated civilly, and it Just Needed To STOP!

And then – I cried. I cried! All my courage outdone by my stupid tears. I felt that I had managed to accomplish the complete opposite of what I set out to do: I wanted to claim my right to be there on equal terms, and instead I had made a fool of myself. I felt small, stupid and humiliated. It was evening and I remember being exhausted from my moment of truth when I went to my room. That's why I didn't get to see the reaction of my classmates until the next morning, when each of them came up to me and apologised. To my surprise, they even thanked me, as they had felt that the tone had turned into something they were also uncomfortable with, but still hadn't done anything to change. None of them commented on my tears. None of them said I was small, stupid, or ridiculous for doing what I did. They saw strength – strength that they talked about for a long time, even outside of our group.

Even so, it took me many years to recognise and acknowledge the strength and courage I displayed when I spoke up about how I felt that day. The fact that I got such a positive response from my classmates the following day failed to make up for my initial reaction. As far as I was concerned, when those tears came out, they were nothing more than a confirmation of my smallness and cowardice.

What I could have done, *should* have done, when I got back to my room after talking to those guys was congratulate myself for having the courage to speak up. I should have acknowledged what I had to overcome to stand up and talk to them in the way that I had; the fact that I was so close to dismissing the problem as something I could just keep accepting, and my own inner dialogue wanting to talk me out of saying anything even until the very last moment. I should have considered all the emotions that had arisen from the experience, and the relief that, at least, I had finally said something. What's more, that next morning I should have taken their comments about how much courage and strength I had displayed to heart, not just focused on their apologies. If I had done that, if I had evaluated what I had done well, it could have served as a source of strength and courage to draw from later in my life. I say that because we can only be deliberate with what we are aware of.

I am sharing this story with you to show you an instance of strength looking completely different from what I had expected it to look like. My experience is that the topics of strength and resilience are articulated in rather 'hard' words in documentaries and books. People talk and write about things like grit and perseverance, about never giving up no matter what, about shutting out their emotions and just getting on with it. This gives rise to visions of soldiers doing drills out in the pouring rain with a drill sergeant shouting into their faces. I don't recognise myself or my strength and resilience in those stories, or any stories couched in that kind of vocabulary. In fact, my response of feeling small and like a coward that day (that seems like a very long time ago as I consider this now), was informed by the kind of narrative that doesn't allow someone who sheds tears to be seen as strong.

These days I realise that the strength I possess and have lived my whole life with is not loud and bold and hard. Instead, it comes from traits that are gentle and quiet and soft. That's why I hadn't even recognised it as strength in myself back in the day. I had been looking for the wrong things. It was almost weird when I think about it now. I knew I was strong, but I never thought real strength looked like, well, me. So even as I was living my strength in a demanding environment working in a high-stakes job, I had been looking around me at all the other strong people I was surrounded by, thinking, "What is it they have that I don't? What am I missing?" That was ever-present in the form of a sort of reservation, or hesitation, I was often stymied by a feeling that I needed to be something 'more' or something 'else'. The idea that being warm, gentle, and happy might be enough was not in my purview.

However, as I started learning more about strength and resilience in my me-search, I arrived at the following conclusion. While I had thought that I was strong *despite* those gentle traits, it turned out that I was strong *because of* them. That was an enormous insight and shift for me, and I came to call these things 'strengths in disguise'. Today I can say that some of my strengths in disguise are being able to actively doubt and reflect, rather than feeling like I need to quickly give a correct answer; seeing failure as a learning experience, and being able to slow down when the pressure is on.

These things might seem counter-intuitive to you, or they might seem very obvious and simple. It depends on how you tend to look at the world and your place within it. In reality, they are probably a bit of both.

What about you? What do your strengths look like? Do you have traits that you don't yet recognise as strengths? I want you to know that when you can identify *your* strengths in disguise, you can draw confidence and motivation from them. That's the difference between feeling like you're just getting by, or maybe you've been lucky, and being able to trust yourself and your capabilities.

Knowing and using your strengths is the difference between just getting by or feeling lucky, and trusting yourself and your capabilities.

When I was interviewing a number of high-performing professional women as part of my 'hiatus project', they gave me several great examples of strengths in disguise. I spoke to women who told me about times when they had taken stances and taken action to create improvement for themselves by setting boundaries or leaving toxic environments. I asked them how strong and confident taking this action and control had made them feel. Interestingly, several of them were surprised at my question because they considered themselves to be weak for notwithstanding the pressure, rather than strong for taking action. Some of them could not even in hindsight be convinced that what they had done displayed strength. From this, I realised, among other things, that I was not the only one with a skewed image of what strength can look like and the expressions it can take.

Let me just say that it would serve us better to recognise when we do things that produce improvements, and remember it for the next time we need to tap into those qualities in ourselves, rather than focusing on the one thing that went wrong. If you make a habit of noticing and evaluating when you do something right or when you overcome some resistance you can build an archive of your own strengths. Refer to this next time you need to do something challenging, as a way to remind yourself that you can do hard things. Below you'll find an exercise on how to do this.

It is also worth noticing that we often give more recognition and compassion to others than we give to ourselves. Practise noticing when you do good things too, and give yourself at least as much compassion as you would give someone else.

EXERCISE ✍

Take a moment now to reflect on situations where you have displayed strength without necessarily realising it. Think back on difficult things you have achieved or difficult situations you have been in, and answer the following questions in the Notes pages at the end of this chapter.
- What was the difficult situation?
- What did you do to improve the situation?
- What internal or external resistance did you have to overcome?
- As you might not always recognise your own strength, even in hindsight, it might help to think "How would I see this situation if it was a friend or colleague who did the same?"

Before moving on, add any other reflections about times you were strong in disguise.

Develop your strengths

The exercise you just did was a way to get you to start looking differently at yourself, at what you have accomplished and how you do things. My hope is that you can see that a shift in perspective is useful when assessing the skills and qualities that you have, and the person you are. Taking part in a quick review like this will give you a basic sense of your abilities and preferences. I invite you to continue to gain an understanding of your strengths because this kind of self-awareness can be a key to both consistent success, and a deeper understanding of yourself.

A talent is an aptitude or ability that comes naturally to you.

It can also be how you most naturally think, feel, and behave. When you use your talents over and over, and spend time developing and practising them, they will develop into strengths.

The thing is, we take our talents for granted and don't necessarily see them for what they are. They are such inherent parts of us that we might make the mistake of thinking that everyone knows how to do the things we can do because of our talents. This is one of the ways we devalue our strength. Since it is so easy for us, we don't prescribe much value to it. If you're like me, you were taught that anything worthwhile requires hard work. It must follow then that if it wasn't hard, if instead it was joyful and put you in a state of flow, it isn't worthwhile or quite enough. This is why simple solutions are often discredited as if harder and more complicated processes would mean a better result.

This is one of the main points I want to make with this book: allow yourself to take what comes easily to you seriously. Allow yourself to see value in simple solutions. Resist the temptation to think that a high degree of complication and difficulty is a measure of value.

> **See the value in the things that come easily for you.**

There are companies that work only with strengths and have excellent tools for assessing and explaining in fine detail what strengths are and how you can learn to use them deliberately. Taking one of their assessments for free or for a small fee can be a first step to unlocking your best potential. I am not affiliated with any of these companies, but I have found them helpful when navigating change. I suggest either www.gallup.com/cliftonstrengths to take their Strength Assessment and discover your top five strengths, or www.strengthsprofile.com to get their free Starter Profile or their paid Introductory Profile. Both services will provide you with a report that lists your top strengths, and information on how you can develop and use your strengths for improved performance and fulfilment.

Knowing your strengths enables you to choose a path of least resistance, a path best suited to the things you are inherently good at. Change can be difficult enough as it is, so it would be wise for you to make it as easy as possible for yourself. Taking action in a way that corresponds to your strengths is a way of smoothing your path forward.

Compile an asset list

In your impressive CV you have a long list of formal accomplishments; academic degrees and other formalised education and training, job positions of increasing importance, honorary positions and roles in organisations of different kinds. From time to time you polish your CV in the hope that someone else will be impressed enough with your achievements to consider you for a new position. When was the last time you considered your CV yourself? When was the last time you had a look at that list of accomplishments you've chalked up purely to reflect on all the things you already have under your belt? The benefit of this is that it will boost your confidence as you allow yourself to be impressed with yourself. You might have never done that. Me neither, not until I had to dust my old CV off and update it when I was forced to think about a different future to the one I assumed I'd have. I think we'd all do well if we let ourselves be impressed by the very things we are wanting others to be impressed by.

EXERCISE

Go ahead now and get out the latest version of your CV. Make any updates needed so that it is current, as you would if you were going to send it out to a recruitment agency.

After you've enjoyed having a good look at your formal accomplishments, I want you to go one step further. I want you to write another list of your 'informal' talents and accomplishments. Maybe you're a good listener, an excellent problem solver, and a great organiser, or always adding a special touch to any gathering, remembering everyone's birthdays and so on. Perhaps you're a mother, a good wife/friend/sister/daughter/neighbour/partner, as well as being a great baker, and fun to be around ... Just keep it coming, all the things you have done that have made you and others happy and that you are even slightly or secretly proud of.

You can also add a third file, with cards and notes and messages from people who have told you how much you mean to them, reminding you of things you have done for them, and how grateful they are to have you in their life.

These compilations together make up your 'Asset List'. They paint a much more comprehensive picture than just your rather sterile CV. It would be great if you were to look at and revel in all the things you are and have done!

Return to this asset list regularly to get used to how awesome you are. Remember the image of your happy, successful future self and start connecting the dots if doubt or uncertainty ever starts to creep in.

Summary

Focus on and develop your strengths rather than your weaknesses.

Unless there are certain specific skills that you need and are lacking, focussing on leveraging your strengths is more worthy of both your time and your effort. The fact is that we all have many strengths of different kinds. When you know what your strengths are you can use them more frequently and more strategically.

Strengths don't always look like you expect them to.

You can only make conscious use of what you are aware of, so becoming aware of your strengths is essential to your success and ability to change.

NOTES

NOTES

Chapter 2

MINDSET

In her book *Mindset* (2006), psychologist Carol S Dweck minted the terms growth mindset and fixed mindset. She described the two different mindsets as different territories, and explained how your environment and experiences will look different depending on which territory you are living in. Let me explain these different mindsets to you.

In the world of **fixed mindsets**, people see intelligence and talent as fixed. It's as if you have what you have in the way of talents because of the capacities you are born with. Therefore, if you are labelled intelligent, talented, or special, you are one of the lucky ones. Success in the world of fixed mindsets is all about proving that you are smart or talented. If you are intelligent and have a fixed mindset, you will spend your time defending that label. You think that if you are as smart as people tell you that you are, you cannot possibly ask questions or tell someone that you don't quite understand something, as that would show your flaws, and people would realise you are not as smart as they thought. So, you'd better play along, pretend you always know everything, and act as if you are always in control.

Can you see how this could stop a person with a fixed mindset from keeping on learning? If there is more to learn, they mustn't know as much as they imagine everyone thinks they do, and their place as one of the lauded ones would be at risk. In the territory of the fixed mindset, people only develop as far as they think they can. Because they don't believe that they can learn and develop for as long as they live, the very thought of their superiority being dented stops people with a fixed mindset from even trying anything they feel is potentially beyond them. That kind of capping of potential to avoid risking failure is one of the limitations of having a fixed mindset. Another limitation is the pressure to keep up appearances. Once they've reached the pinnacle, they don't want to risk falling off it.

On the other hand, in the territory of the **growth mindset**, people know that they can always learn and develop. In fact, stretching yourself and learning new things is what constitutes success in this territory. Curiosity, a thirst for learning, and a willingness to try new things can make anything possible. With a growth mindset you know that failure is part of learning, you are not afraid of asking questions, and you are open to new ideas. You might have started with less talent or intelligence than someone who went straight up on their pedestal in the world of the fixed mindset, but the way people operate in growth mindset territory means that as soon as they surpass one pinnacle, they are off to learn more and strive for greater things. For people with a growth mindset, there are always new goals to work towards.

The same people that the person with a fixed mindset was afraid to ask for help or advice because she didn't want to forego the opportunity to impress them with her specialness, and/or risk losing face, are always more than happy to help. What's more, they won't see the slightest sign of weakness or lack in the person asking the questions. What they'll see instead is the drive, engagement and limitless potential of someone eager to learn and grow. Can you see how these two mindsets create different "worlds" for the people who have them? We generally live our life out in one of these territories most of the time, but we can express the traits that are characteristic of the other mindset in certain areas of our life, or certain situations. Think about where you're positioned; do you mostly see limitations, or do you see possibilities? In the next chapter, you will learn how you can start to shift yourself out of a fixed mindset if you recognise that you're being limited by it.

> **Whether you have a fixed or a growth mindset determines how you show up in your life.**

Curiosity is one of my highest values. I have always loved learning and I'm not overly afraid of failure. What that means is that I generally live in the world of a growth mindset. Except that is, sometimes in relation to the biggest part of my life for many years – flying.

Flying is something that often impresses people. The world of aviation seems to represent a mix of excitement, exclusiveness, luxury and superiority, and the people working within it get to personify those traits. It was already clear to me that it was considered a special thing to do when I was applying for admission into the flying school. The fact that there are so few women in the industry (even if that was something I rarely considered myself), made people think it was an even more special achievement of mine to become a pilot. It was that wow! again.

I came to this realisation about my own experience when I read Dweck's book on mindset. To a certain extent the fact that people thought it was special that I was a pilot rubbed off on me, and I sometimes found myself in a fixed mindset, in situations where what I needed most was a growth mindset. As far as the day-to-day requirements of my job went, I certainly used my growth mindset most of the time. I was always wanting to learn more and get a better understanding of the dimensions of the role by regularly asking my colleagues if they had encountered any situations that I could learn from. Meanwhile, there were times when that unconscious sense of 'specialness' stopped me from asking for help for fear of showing a lack of knowledge that I felt I should already have. It was crazy really. I would spend hours with my nose in manuals finding the answer to something that one of my colleagues would have been able to fill me in on in a matter of minutes.

It's particularly helpful to operate from a growth mindset when we are navigating our way through change. I promise that it will be easier if you stay open and curious, and don't hesitate to ask people for help so that you can learn from their knowledge and experience. You will find that it is a recurring theme in this book to stay open to new learnings, new ways of doing things, and new ideas.

Change means that you will have to either do things differently, or do different things. You are making it harder for yourself, not easier, if you think you already know everything you need to know. Learning from people who know more than you is smart. It is also a lot more fun than doing everything on your own. There is no need to invent the wheel again. I needed to lean into my curiosity again and again on my own journey through change. I didn't hold back when it came to reaching out to people who had done what I wanted to do to learn about things like how to write and publish a book, how to start and market a company, etc. I suggest that you too make the most of other people's experiences, and fast-track your transformation and growth in the process with the right help from the right people.

EXERCISE ✍

In the pages ahead, journal on the following questions:
- Do you mostly display a fixed or a growth mindset?
- Is there a certain area of your life where, or certain times when, you display the other type of mindset?
- How is this helping or hindering you?
- What can you do to create a shift if necessary?

Summary

A fixed mindset is one where you see the level of intelligence and talents you have as fixed, and there is not much room for further learning.

A growth mindset is one where you know that you can always learn and improve.

The kind of mindset you have affects how you see yourself and the world you live in.

We generally have either a fixed or a growth mindset but can express traits of the other in certain situations or at certain times.

NOTES

Chapter 3

A HEAD FULL OF THOUGHTS

Everything we do starts with a thought.

A recent study carried out in 2020 showed that we have more than 6,000 thoughts a day. I sure don't know how to identify where one thought ends and the next one begins, but I guess the researchers have developed a way to do that. What are all those thoughts then? I pose that question here because I am interested in both the physiology of thoughts and the content of the thoughts that take up time and space in our minds. As thoughts are behind the decisions we make and the way we feel, I think it is useful to have an understanding of exactly what thoughts are.

If everything we do starts with a thought, it follows that when we need to do things differently to get a different result, we have to be open to thinking differently. To do that we first need to become aware of the thoughts we are thinking. It sounds easy enough I know, but as much as 95 percent of our brain's activity is unconscious. It takes some conscious effort on our part to become aware of our thoughts and any patterns they follow.

This chapter covers the question of what a thought is, and what a thought does inside the body. Having a basic understanding of this is helpful in several ways. Firstly, separating yourself from your thoughts will help you become more aware of them. This in turn will help you identify your thought patterns. This is important because awareness is crucial to our ability to change our habits.

Secondly, knowing what a thought is demystifies it. On a physical level, a thought is a concrete signal inside your body, not something ethereal. Having that one piece of information alone makes it easier to understand how it is that what we think affects how we feel, and therefore how it colours our life.

Because after all, you are the only thinker in your head.

Think about that for a moment. Everything that is going on in that mind of yours right now; the to-do-lists on endless repeat, the plans you are making, the rehashing of problems and doubting your ability to solve them, the memories that keep you stuck, and the thoughts that make you happy, are all down to you. In other words, if there are thoughts in your head right now, it is because of you, and only you. You are the only one thinking them and therefore you are the only one keeping them active in your mind. You are also the only one who can stop thinking them. And that, right there, is your point of power. I say that because there's nothing stopping you from choosing to stop thinking thoughts you don't want to think.

You are the only thinker in your head.

Can you imagine what your life would be like if you only chose to think thoughts that are helpful to you? Getting to that state starts with awareness of the thoughts you are currently thinking, and applying conscious effort to interrupt the habitual thought patterns that have developed over the years until your brain has had time to learn new more helpful thought patterns. Getting you there is what this chapter is about.

Become aware of your thoughts

Becoming aware of your thoughts is key to your transformation and growth because (as you've heard before) you can only change the things you are aware of. You can start to create a habit of metacognition (i.e. the practice of awareness of your own thoughts) by following the suggestions below.

As most of our thoughts are unconscious, and many of our conscious thoughts are automated, you will have to make a conscious effort to become aware of them at any given moment. Catch yourself in different situations and make a mental note of what thoughts are going through your head. Also, notice the language you are using. Is it positive and encouraging, or is it critical, judgemental, and berating? Are you using the same language whether you are thinking about yourself and your actions, or somebody else and their actions? If it is a different voice, which voice is friendlier?

If you do this several times a day you will start to see patterns. It might be helpful to link this practice to a habit you have already established. For example, what is your mind thinking when you are going about your daily habits like brushing your teeth, unpacking the dishwasher, driving to work, etc? Alternatively, you could link it to a certain state by noticing what your thoughts are in situations where you tend to get nervous, frustrated or stressed.

EXERCISE

Expand your metacognition by catching your thoughts often during the day, and write what you notice down, either as you go along or when you can sit down and reflect for a few moments. That way you can start hearing your inner voice and vocabulary and start seeing the patterns that are playing out. There is no need to analyse the thoughts that you encounter; this exercise is simply to create awareness of what they are.

The physiology of a thought

A thought is an electrochemical signal that is channelled through a network of neurons in your brain. This is my layman's attempt at describing what a thought does in your body and brain: Like a Mexican wave, it starts with an input at one end and gets transferred through a long strand of neurons to a place where it triggers a response. This could be a muscle movement or a hormonal response of some kind. The sequence of neurons involved in each particular thought depends on many things. If it is a familiar thought, the pathway is already laid down in your brain, and the message is transmitted with less effort and more speed. If the thought is new and unfamiliar it has to find its way through your neural networks. You might meet resistance when you are thinking a new thought as your brain, mind and body don't yet know where it belongs because there is no established neural pathway for it.

You can think about building new neural pathways (by way of thinking new thoughts and learning new things) like this: Imagine that there is a meadow of tall grass ahead of you. To get to the other side for the first time you are going to have to walk through the tall grass. If you turn around and look behind you when you reach the other side, chances are there will be no (or very little) trace of you ever having been there. Next time you have to walk across the same meadow you'll have to look hard to be able to find the route you took the last time. However, each time you walk across the meadow the route becomes easier to find because over time you have incrementally created a clearer path.

This is not unlike the process that goes on in your brain when you learn something new or start thinking in new ways. At first everything is unfamiliar, and you have to concentrate and think consciously about every step you take. With more practice, each step becomes easier, smoother, and quicker as the new neural pathways first connect, and then strengthen. You've probably heard that it takes a specific amount of time to form a new habit, but there is no consensus on how long that is, with the results from different studies ranging from 20 days to 254 days.

What matters more than the specific amount of time, is how often and how many times you practice. These two factors will decide how quickly the new neural pathway is developed, which represents how quickly you learn your new skill or form a new habit that sticks.

Thinking a new thought requires conscious effort until it is automated.

Eventually, you will be able to apply your new skill or habit without needing to concentrate because it will be automated. Think back to when you learnt to drive; everything was complicated in the beginning. There were so many things to think about and learn, and now you drive around without much thinking at all.

I bet you've even arrived home sometimes without being able to remember how you got there. This is because your brain has built strong neural pathways and hence automated the skill of driving a car. That means you don't need to engage the executive part of the brain to do it, and there is still plenty of brain energy left over for other things, like reacting instantly to that bike rider that swerved in front of you out of nowhere, for example. Luckily, thanks to the strong, automated neural pathway, there was spare energy and capacity to deal with a threat like that much better than you would have when you first learnt to drive.

To go back to basics, your brain's most fundamental task is to direct energy to keep you alive. It has a few different strategies to do this in a way that spends as little energy as possible to ensure your survival in the short term. Automating your thoughts and actions is one of the main ways your brain does this. Once a thought pattern or action pattern is automated by being repeated enough times, it is stored in a part of the brain that doesn't require as much energy and processing power as cognitive thought does. This is the most energy-efficient way for the brain to function. It's a matter of pure logistics. Anything new and different will require more energy from your brain and hence initially meet resistance. What's more, your brain knows that whatever you have been doing so far has kept you alive so it is obviously safe, in the brain's immediate survival way of operating. More of the same is energy efficient and safe. New things will take effort and energy, and potentially pose a risk.

The physiology of your brain has no morals or judgement. It makes no difference to your brain what it automates and stores away. For you and me that means that our brain stores away 'bad' habits just as easily as 'good' habits. This is one of the reasons we should pay attention to what patterns we repeat and therefore automate.

The soundtrack in our head

I am the only thinker in my head.

That is something I often remind myself of. It gives me power, responsibility, and agency. It snaps me 'out of it' when I am stuck. It reminds me that I have the ability to choose a different more helpful thought to get unstuck. It helps me focus on the solution rather than the problem. Sometimes this is confronting, as it forces me to take responsibility for the times I wallow in non-helpful thoughts, like pettiness, judgement, blame or victimhood. I'm grateful for this reminder because over the years it has brought me a lot of awareness of the thoughts in my head and kept me accountable for their consequences. I have learnt to see both the immediate effect of choosing a different thought, and the wider effects on my life as I have calibrated my mind's filter, which you will read about later in this chapter.

The soundtrack in my head took on a different tune when I got dumped by that metaphorical wave after my eye 'broke'. The whole situation was so new to me that I didn't have any points of reference at all. Among other things, I felt so confused about what was happening to me, not to mention what might happen moving forward. I didn't know how far my vision would deteriorate or how much pain it would cause me along the way. There was a lot that I could not control about the situation I was in, but there was one thing I was able to take control over: the thoughts in my head. After tumbling around in that wave for a while, with my mind focussed on worst-case scenarios, I realised taking control of the narrative inside my head was the first critical step to getting back in control of my own agenda.

> *Take control of the soundtrack in your head, and make it play a helpful tune.*

In our early life, learning comes from the outside. When we are little, we are wide open to all the impressions and stimuli around us. From the very beginning of our lives, we mimic, observe, and listen to everything in our environment. That is how we learn anything and everything, and when we know nothing, we take everything in. This serves us well because it's the way we learn to walk and talk, socialise, and basically, survive. At some point, our learning goes beyond mere survival as we learn more intricate skills and facts. We start to notice that different people do things differently, and we start to ask questions that elicit responses that are coloured by the perspective of the person giving them.

At some stage, we reach a point in our development where we no longer need to be wide open to everything people around us say and do. We can start to vet the input we receive and consider whether the advice we are being given is founded in a fact or an opinion. In the case of the latter, we can then choose whether we want to accept that advice or disregard it. However, it seems to me that we have not been taught that we can close those floodgates that have, by necessity, been wide open, and instead take charge of what we let come into our conscious awareness.

What I'm getting at here is that we aren't really taught to think about thinking. That is unfortunate because the ability to apply meta-thinking is a powerful thing to possess. I say that because awareness of our thoughts is essential for any transformation and growth to take place.

If you are like me and just about everyone else on the planet, your mind is rarely or never silent. There is a constant soundtrack playing in the background. It is an eternal flow of big and small thoughts around important and unimportant stuff. I'm sure you know what I'm talking about. It is an inner dialogue made up of knowledge and beliefs. A belief comes about through the acceptance that something is true even without (or maybe especially without) proof. When we had the floodgates of our mind wide open when we were learning about the world as a child, a lot of what we took onboard were other people's beliefs. Beliefs can turn out to be facts, but it doesn't matter whether they are facts or not, because as long as we hold on to them and don't dig any further to ascertain their merit, they are a powerful force in the way our life plays out. That's because beliefs inform our assumptions about ourselves and the world we live in. Some of these beliefs are true and some aren't. Some are empowering and others limit us. We don't usually question them, maybe because we are not even aware of them on account of our assumption that we are living an objective truth, or perhaps it's just because we don't see any reason to question them.

Take inventory of your beliefs.

I think it should be part of every adult's life to take inventory of their thoughts and beliefs from time to time. Unfortunately, it usually takes some kind of a crisis or breakdown, or some big turning point to initiate a journey of self-development for people to learn that they can not only take an inventory of what is already going on in their head but also take charge of what they let into it in the future.

At some point, it is up to us to take control and responsibility over who we *actually* are in order to become the person we want to be. Can you see now that there is in fact a lot you can do about what goes on in your mind, and take responsibility for how you interpret and use it?

Our beliefs are often generalisations and/or exaggerations, and as such may include words like 'always', 'never', 'everyone', and 'no one'. When the voice in your head is giving you reasons to do or not do something using these words, warning bells should be ringing. You should see it as a sign to stop and ask yourself if it is a fact or a belief you're hearing. The voice in your head might say, "People like me always/never …" (for example "People like me never get the top job").

EXERCISE

Take your thought through these three steps:
1. Is this thought a fact or a belief? Is it factually true that people in exactly my situation, with exactly my strengths and weaknesses, traits, experiences etc every single time … / or not even once has … ?
2. Is this a conclusion that I have drawn myself, or is it someone else's belief that I am unwittingly carrying around?
3. Is this thought helpful?

The point of this exercise is twofold. Firstly, it will make you aware of times when you are telling yourself things that aren't true, and secondly, it will remind you that you don't have to think thoughts that aren't helpful. You are the only thinker in your head! That means it's up to you to discard any old thought patterns that no longer serve you.

The brain-body connection

Think of a big juicy lemon that weighs heavily in your hand as you hold it; that's how juicy it is. Imagine you cut it in half and see the juice as it drips out of it. Cut a wedge and imagine putting it in your mouth and biting down as your mouth fills with the sour lemon juice. Can you taste it? Can you feel it in your mouth? I bet you can. You might have even salivated as you read this, or perhaps you cringed a little bit and puckered your lips at the thought of the sour lemon juice in your mouth.

What this exercise demonstrates is the fact that our thoughts are responsible for the sensations we feel in our bodies. As you've just experienced, thinking about lemon juice triggered a chemical reaction because the brain and body cannot distinguish between a vividly imagined event and a real one. That's why the act of imagining lemon juice in your mouth can elicit the same or a similar bodily response it would if your mouth was actually filled with lemon juice.

What you think has physical effects on your body.

This is a simple illustration of the effects of our thoughts. I want you to keep it in mind as you read this book. In fact, I want you to always keep it in mind, because in the same way as they can trigger a physical response when we imagine a lemon, any thought can make you feel good or uneasy. Put simply, a thought will cause the activation of a whole symphony of activity in your body, and the way you end up feeling depends on the balance between your body's stress response and your body's feel-good response.

I share all of this with you because you will benefit from being equipped with the understanding that thoughts create real physical responses in your body. This is important when we are talking about how your brain works to keep you safe by triggering the stress response, and what you can do to let your brain know that you have the situation under control. After all, in a healthy mental state, you are in charge of your brain, not the other way around. Our ability to respond to stressful and threatening situations is essential for our survival. However, what constitutes a stressful situation is different for all of us. Something that is exciting to someone might be terrifying to someone else. This is because when your brain is deciding whether a situation is a threat or not, it draws on past experience and the unconscious programming you develop as you move through your life. Your comfort zone is comfortable because it doesn't cause any big and unpleasant fluctuations in your body's physiology. Automated thoughts and behaviours enable you to get through a lot of your life on autopilot, and as such, they are energy efficient and safe as far as the brain is concerned. However, when you approach the edges of your comfort zone your brain needs to decide whether it's safe to step beyond it, or whether getting out of your comfort zone represents too much of a threat to your safety under the circumstances at hand.

Recent research suggests that the brain is a prediction machine that regulates its activity according to predictions it makes based on previous experience. When it comes to something that involves getting out of our comfort zone, for example, it would recall how much of a threat a similar situation posed in the past, and consider how well we coped with that situation. If we coped alright, then our body would know that it doesn't need to hit the big alarm button, and vice versa. Now that you know about this, you have the opportunity to change your reactions to the things that happen on a day-to-day basis by catching yourself when you start feeling the physical discomfort of the unknown, and rather than retreating to habitual reactions based on fear, you can consciously assess the situation and choose a different reaction that doesn't limit your options in the way that fear does. That's how you can start stretching your comfort zone, which is incredibly helpful when it comes to being able to change. You'll be hearing more about this shortly when I show you how to easily change your state with small steps.

Keep returning to the juicy lemon as a reminder that your thoughts influence how you feel.

EXERCISE

This is an exercise to make you aware of how your thoughts feel in your body.

Start by thinking about a time when you had to overcome resistance of some kind and you wound up doing really well. Or perhaps there was a time when you got a level of praise or recognition. Remember that moment in as much detail as possible, taking note of where you were, who else was there, what the scene around you looked like, what you could hear, etc. Close your eyes and be there in that moment. How does that make you feel?

Next, think of a situation when something went wrong. Perhaps there was a time when you embarrassed yourself or made a mistake of some kind with negative consequences. Try to return to that moment with as much detail as possible. How does revisiting this experience make you feel?

Are you able to notice a difference in your body between the two different scenarios? Was it maybe even difficult for you to think back in detail to the negative scenario?

Earlier in this chapter, you did an exercise to make yourself aware of your thoughts throughout the day. Now I want you to add another layer to this awareness by considering what feelings your thoughts are producing. So, when you catch yourself thinking, notice the feeling you feel in your body. Identify the thoughts that make you feel more energised, calm, frustrated, restless, etc. Then experiment by choosing a different thought and observing if it changes the feeling in your body.

Now here is a question that will really move the needle: Do you think you can use the knowledge of this brain-body connection to recognise when you are getting close to the edge of your comfort zone, and instead of pulling back, let yourself take the step forward?

You will see what you think of

Look around you right now and take a mental snapshot that includes all of your senses. That snapshot would include innumerable shapes, colours, sounds, smells, impressions, and people and objects, both familiar and unfamiliar. It wouldn't even be possible for your senses to pick up all the input coming at you at any given moment. Consider how many snapshots like that you could take in a day and try to imagine the volume of data that surrounds you every day. It is enormous! There can be up to 2,000,000 bits of data coming at us at any one time. Our brain cannot process that much information, so it needs a way to filter the information to be able to handle it. It does this through its own selective filtering and attention processes, in which your brain automatically deselects information it doesn't deem important for your survival or thriving in the short term. Next, your brain value tags the information it has taken in, in order of importance. There is both a logical and an emotional aspect to this value tagging, where your brain takes your previous experiences and reactions into account when deciding the value of something.

When I learnt about this process in a course on applied neuroscience, I immediately thought about how the algorithms on search engines and social media work in terms of giving us more of what we have already searched for. You look at something once and ads for the same or similar products keep popping up for weeks. Basically, our brain does the same thing when it tags the things we pay attention to again and again as important, and lets more of those things through while filtering other things out.

The reason I'm sharing this with you is that it is important to know that your brain selectively ignores a lot of the information that comes at you all day long. Meanwhile, it lets through the information that you have a record of paying attention to. It is up to you to consciously prime your brain to notice and pay attention to information and opportunities that are in your best interest. 'Consciously' is the keyword here.

Did you know that 95 percent of the thoughts you have today are the same thoughts you had yesterday, and the same thoughts you will have tomorrow unless you pay conscious attention to what's going on and start choosing different thoughts? This is important because the thoughts you think create the emotions you feel. Therefore, they co-create the state your body is in and make up the habits you live with that ultimately shape your life.

Unless you become aware of what your thoughts are, you have very little scope to control your life.

> **The thoughts you think create the emotions you feel.**

The self-talk that is the soundtrack in your mind, becomes part of the filter and the value tagging your brain uses to present you with information from all the inputs constantly coming at you. Like your computer's algorithm, your brain gives you more of what you are constantly thinking of on the assumption that it must be important to you. The more you think about something, the more you notice it around you. You take this as 'proof' that you were right – and round and round it goes.

In a sense, you are living a self-fulfilling prophecy. What you see is not the world how it is, but the world how *you* are. Remember, your brain filters in more, not of what you want, but of what you focus on.

> **Your brain filters in more of what you focus on.**

That's why it is important to focus on what you want, not on what you don't want.

It's easier said than done though, because we are also affected by something called the negativity bias. This is a propensity that humans have to focus more on negative events and experiences than positive ones. We also respond more strongly to, and more readily recall and remember things that have gone badly for us. The negativity bias is said to amplify negative experiences

2.5 times more than positive ones. What this means is that we have to consciously make up for this bias by upscaling our focus on positive experiences.

You might know someone who is thought of as being 'lucky'. That someone seems to get opportunities others don't. They always seem to be in the right place at the right time, catch any breaks that are there to be caught, and just seem to live a charmed life. Let's consider that person more closely for a moment; think about their general demeanour and attitude, as well as the words they use, and the choices they make. I think you will find that person to be a positive person who smiles more than they frown, sees possibilities and opportunities rather than problems, and is not afraid to step up and have a crack at the opportunities. My guess is that they are also grateful and easygoing, have a can-do attitude, and don't get bogged down in worries and negativity. The mindset and attitude of your 'lucky' friend filter through to the experiences they have, and the results they get.

A person who, on the other hand, sees everything as difficult, probably looks at other people who seem to 'have it easy' with suspicion, or they think others are selfish and out to get them. These kinds of people are simply not open to the same kinds of opportunities that the 'lucky' people take advantage of. It's not that the same opportunity isn't available to them, it's that they are so affected by their own negative filter that they just don't see it when it comes their way. If they do see it, they're likely to think it's too good to be true, or they'll think that it isn't the right time for them to take advantage of it, or find some other reason to justify saying no to the opportunity. And so, it passes them by, and they keep considering themselves to be unlucky.

If you have a look behind the words 'Lucky' and 'Unlucky' I am certain you will find a number of behaviours that indicate what outcome each person will come to expect and therefore get. Each little thought we think, and keep thinking, becomes part of the filter that we see the world through. This means that the world will look different depending on what our filter is made up of.

A person called Lucky and another one called Unlucky could stand right next to each other without a lot telling them apart until someone asks the question, "Who is willing to try?" Lucky will say, "I am! This could be interesting, I wonder what I will learn," and Unlucky will say "Not a chance, they are just out to get you. Besides, this isn't a good time for me now anyway". Essentially both of them will have their viewpoints affirmed and their filters will remain in place. Lucky will end up with a new experience that might lead to exciting new things, and even if the experience turns out to be less than great, their attitude will include appreciation for the fact that they will have at least learnt something from it, and they will be able to let it go and move on. Meanwhile, Unlucky will also have their filter confirmed; they will stay firm in their conviction that you always have to be on your guard because people want to take advantage of you, and that nothing exciting ever happens to them. I see this happening around me all the time. I bet you do too.

Pause and think of the successful people around you. Are they lucky – or positive, open, curious, and willing to give things a go? Are they unlucky – or overly cautious, suspicious, full of excuses and afraid of failure? I can't guarantee you a lotto win, but I can guarantee that you will become a lot 'luckier' if you open yourself up to opportunities. If you don't just read this book, but also take action on what you learn from reading it, you will be able to recalibrate your filters so that you too can be one of the so-called 'lucky' people.

> *Calibrate your filter to notice the things you want in your life.*

Imagine a light switch that you have sole control of. You can choose to turn that switch on and live in the light or turn it off and live in the dark. That switch does not control the people and things that go on around you, however, people and things will look different when you can see them clearly because they are in the light. What's more, even if you cannot control who comes into your life, you know that simply having your light on will keep certain people and activities at bay. It doesn't deny that there is darkness outside the distance your light can illuminate. It doesn't deny that life looks different in the dark. It also can't change the fact that tough things happen sometimes. It just makes it easier and more pleasant for you to go about living your life as an active participant. It also puts you in a better position to reach further into the unknown when you are ready. How empowering is it to know that at any moment you can choose your thoughts and your focus? What do you choose to focus on? Do you focus on the smiles of strangers you pass on your way to work each morning or the frowns of other busy commuters? Do you focus on the driver that lets you in when you're trying to change lanes or the one that cuts you off? Do you focus on the fact that the restaurant you went to for lunch had your second choice or the fact that they didn't have your first? Do you focus on the compliments you get for a job well done or the one point for improvement that came with the feedback you were being offered?

> *In every moment you can choose your thoughts and your focus.*

As you can see, there are endless little moments every day where we have the choice to focus on the positive or the negative, the solution or the problem. Each little choice programs our filter, which lets in more of the same. This matters because these little choices turn into habits that turn us into the people we are.

It all starts with a thought.

EXERCISE

What are your filters? Consider what you have discovered about your thoughts as you've been reading this book, and how those thoughts influence the filter through which you see the world.

Have your thought patterns changed at all since you started becoming aware of them, and found out that it is up to you to change them if they are making you less resourceful? Can you see that how you see the world and the people around you is up to you?

On the Notes pages at the end of this chapter write a few reflections on what you've noticed about the way you are thinking about your own thinking (i.e. your metacognition), and how this is affecting you.

Create a new soundtrack

So far in this chapter, you have learnt that:

- You are the only thinker in your head.
- Your brain loves automating thoughts as this saves energy.
- When you were a child, you had 'open doors' to your brain to take in everything that you needed to learn.

- When you got older those doors were still open and let in a lot of information that you weren't aware you could choose to take on board or not.
- A lot of what made it in and became part of your filter turns out not to be fact but other peoples' opinions and fears, resulting in you walking around playing a never-ending soundtrack in your mind made up (in part) of other peoples' opinions, values and advice.

You have also learnt that you can only make conscious use of what you are aware of. You have done several exercises to become aware of the thoughts you are thinking as you've moved through this chapter. Make no mistake about it, now is the time for you to discard any thoughts you no longer want, and create a new soundtrack made up of more resourceful thoughts that will empower you to get to where you want to be.

Your new soundtrack needs to be helpful rather than cheerful, and it should be tailored to your own needs. So, take some time to consider what's going to be helpful for you. Do you need to be nurtured and encouraged? Or do you need to be challenged and pushed? Do you need to remind yourself to operate from your 'haves' rather than your 'have-nots'? What phrases, said in what tone, would be helpful for you to have playing inside your head? I encourage you to give yourself that.

Create a soundtrack that is helpful to you.

Once you have created your new soundtrack, you need to reinforce it by practising it. Remember that how often you practice determines how long it will take to create a new neural pathway. It's not about how many days go by. It's about reminding yourself that it's the new thought pattern that you want to embed over and over again until it becomes automated. Know that every time you actively turn to your new soundtrack, you are walking one more lap through that tall grass in the meadow of your brain, widening the path as you're strengthening your new neural connections. Little by little it will be easier and eventually become automatic for you to approach every day with conscious and helpful self-talk.

EXERCISE

Now it's your turn. Creating a new conscious soundtrack that is playing in the back of your mind will completely change your life. Fill it with words and phrases that bring out the best in you, and you'll see an improvement in both your performance and your mood. It's important to be picky with the words and images that you use.

Start by writing down five sentences that you want to be part of your new soundtrack and get used to saying them over and over in your head. You can take it a step further and record yourself saying these sentences, and listen to them as you exercise, do your chores, and generally go about your day. The very act of writing, talking, and listening activates different networks in your brain and will create a bigger imprint. Hearing your own voice saying empowering things will make a big difference to your outlook. Frequent repetition is what it takes to make your new soundtrack automatic.

This is not negotiable because your old soundtrack has been playing on repeat in your head for many years and its pathways are well established. It is not that difficult to change tracks per se, but it will require conscious awareness to kick things off. Bits and pieces of the old one will keep coming back until the new one has had enough repetitions to take over. Don't let the fact that this will take time and effort stop you. When you catch yourself playing your old soundtrack, just remember that you are no longer listening to that tune because you have a new and better version to listen to now.

You might find it helpful to also write down a few sentences that you see as warning signs. They might be limiting beliefs that you have become aware of through this process. All you need to do when you hear these sentences as part of your self-talk is remember to bring yourself back to a more resourceful place by remembering more helpful thoughts.

What to do with worrying

We all have problems and worries to deal with from time to time. They must not be ignored or dismissed, nor can they be solved by simply turning to a new empowering soundtrack. I don't propose glossing over things that are difficult or worrisome. However, you don't need to let your problems and worries eat you up by going on constant repeat in your mind. Here are two strategies to give your worries the attention they need, but no more than that.

1. Deal with them right away. Make that phone call, ask that question, pay that bill, sit down and make a plan; whatever it is you need to do to resolve (or start resolving) your problem; or –
2. Set aside a time each day that you quarantine as your 'Worry Time'. Then when things pop into your head during the day,

tell yourself "I'll deal with that at Worry Time". This way you are not dismissing the worries, but you are saving the energy you would otherwise be burning through mulling over them endlessly. When the clock strikes Worry Time take out a pen and a notepad and get to work. Which of the worries involve problems you can deal with? Take action on the actual, practical things and you will significantly lessen the load.

> **Setting up a Worry Time frees up your thinking the rest of the time.**

General worries often shrink when you look at them square on. Giving them some undivided attention for the 15 minutes or so that you treat as Worry Time is a good way to free up head space during the rest of the day. This is not about dismissing things that are bothering you, it's about not mulling over your worries all day, turning big problems into small ones, and avoiding procrastinating about things you can do something about.

Summary

This has been a big chapter with a lot of information for you to take on board about what thoughts are, how they came into your head, and what they are doing in your body. These are some key points to keep in mind:

Your brain loves automating thoughts because it is a way for it to conserve energy and keep you alive. This is your brain's main job.

The thoughts in your head are a never-ending stream of facts and beliefs, memories and predictions based on your experiences and mindset.

A lot of the beliefs you carry around are the result of comments, opinions and advice from other people that might or might not be true, and might or might not serve you. It is your privilege and your responsibility to choose the thoughts you think, otherwise they will choose you based on what you've got going on in your head.

Your thoughts affect the filter that lets in new information from all of the inputs around you. Like the algorithms of your computer, your brain lets through more of what you are already focussing on. This is how your thought patterns get confirmed, and around and around it goes.

To notice new things, you need to start thinking new thoughts.

You can create a soundtrack that is deliberate, conscious and helpful by deciding what you would like to hear inside your head.

NOTES

NOTES

NOTES

Chapter 4

EMBRACE THE REST OF YOU

What I want you to do here is pause for a moment to take stock of how far we've come. Remember that we're still in the first part of the book, which is all about assessing what you already have. We started by looking at the power of knowing and developing your strengths, and we got to see how this leads to more productivity as well as more fulfilment. You not only got to consider several different ways of looking at strengths, but you also compiled a comprehensive asset list.

You then learned about the concepts of fixed and growth mindsets before we dove into the question of what thoughts are, and how to empower yourself by creating a helpful soundtrack to have playing in the back of your mind.

The aim of this part of the book is to get you to a place where you can see all that you have rather than what you don't have, and live from a position of strength rather than weakness. A key benefit of this approach is that when you look at yourself this way you will feel empowered. This makes changing any aspect of your life that is not working for you a real possibility.

Therefore, in the process of becoming all that you are, it is time to embrace your shortcomings just as readily as embracing your strengths. Your so-called failures, your embarrassments and your poor decisions – embrace them all. I want you to see that approaching life in this way, along with having a growth mindset and a helpful soundtrack playing in the background, allows room for you to feel good about yourself while embracing the things that you might have previously wanted to hide.

Not only that; there is an even more powerful reason for you to embrace all that you are, and that is that when you accept the parts of yourself that you are not proud of, they lose the grip they have on you. You no longer have to hide them, you no longer have to make excuses for, or defend them, and they no longer have the power to trigger or threaten you. It is not necessary to make a public display of your mess or wear it as a badge of honour. All you need to do is accept it. This is important because when you accept your shadows, no one can leverage them against you. Another benefit is that when you accept your perceived shortcomings they will more or less shrink into insignificance.

You are your biggest asset.

Embracing all of me

One thing that I never used to know what to make of is my introversion. Extroversion and introversion are terms that pertain to the way people get their energy. Socialising and being amongst people is a way to recharge their energy for extroverts, while introverts recharge by spending time alone or in close conversations with one, or at most a few people. Introversion is often misunderstood as shyness, and therefore it is generally seen as a less desirable trait than extroversion.

I have always been very aware of my need for solitude to recharge. That need was very well met when I got to spend a lot of time on my own on overnight trips when I was a pilot. It gave me time to rest, reset, reflect, and do all the things I needed to perform at my best at work and at home.

I used to think of myself as a lone wolf. I wasn't shy, I just wasn't very interested in being among crowds of people. During a time of reflection when I was getting ready to write this book, I looked my introversion in the eye and decided I was strong enough to call it by its real name. Once I did that, I was able to embrace it and see it as an asset because it makes me good at reflecting and assessing situations from several perspectives. It is also an asset when it comes to making connections, rather than simply making contacts. This matters to me because I am much more interested in the person I am talking to, not what goes on around us.

When I worked as a pilot, I knew that I was living and working from my strength every day. I have already shared with you that even so, I didn't always recognise what strength consisted of. Recognising and embracing my introversion, I realised that it is possible to be strong and soft at the same time, and I could see that there were no missing pieces. It was the fact that I hadn't fully embraced my introversion, not my introversion itself, that showed up as a hesitation. I can't help but wonder how things might have been if I had known myself better in those days.

Are you, like me, strong, high performing, and capable, while at the same time also quiet, gentle, and introverted? If so, I want you to know that it is possible to be all of these things. There is no contradiction in having the so-called powerful qualities, as well as soft and gentle qualities at the same time. There is no missing link. You don't have to look for something else outside of yourself to complete the picture. The qualities introverts like us possess can actually equate to a superpower.

EXERCISE ✍

It is time for you to embrace your apparent shortcomings. Be brave and honest, and on the pages at the end of this chapter, or on a piece of paper, write down some of the things that you are less proud of, embarrassed about, or normally try to hide from others and yourself. The reason I suggest the option of writing this down on a piece of paper rather than on the pages ahead is that you might feel freer to let them out if it feels less permanent. This might remove some resistance as you go about this task.

You might find that these perceived shortcomings lose their bite simply by appearing as words on a page. Or maybe you will find that they have faded over time, and something you've carried around for a long time as an embarrassment, actually means little or nothing to you now.

I then want to invite you to go further into your own shadow and think back on a time when you got frustrated, angry or very uncomfortable. Consider what you weren't getting at that moment when those feelings were coming up. What need, that you wouldn't normally admit to anyone (maybe not even yourself), wasn't being met? Where you start feeling that icky or naughty feeling, that's where you need to go in your mind. Chances are that you may not have even been aware that this was a problem for you at the time. However, if you can stay in that space now, despite the discomfort you might be feeling, and identify the word or words to describe what you were secretly wishing you had in that situation when you got so frustrated, you will have found a key to making it a lot easier to move beyond some of the limiting beliefs that could be holding you back from taking action on your goals.

This is the world of our shadow. It is the place where the things we want to keep hidden because of the icky or guilty feeling that comes with them, are stored. It is often the same thing that annoys us when we see it in other people. Why don't you take a moment now to think about a person who has this annoying quality? Can you name that quality? If you can, ask yourself, "Where in my life would I like to have more of that quality?" If nothing jumps out at you in the way of an answer to that question, ask yourself, "Where in my life does this quality turn up in my behaviour?"

Once you find that word or words that live below the icky/guilty feeling, sit with them for a while and think about whether there's a way to see the benefit of you having these traits. It might help to find a person you admire who owns this same trait in a positive way.

Now that your assessment of all that you are is complete, and you realise that you are allowed to be all of that, you can probably see that in fact, you are only at your best when you are all of that.

Summary

You are the best version of yourself when you are all that you are. It might sound like a contradiction in terms, but adding the things you might have thought of as minuses in the past, will increase the total sum of you. They do not subtract from it. Embracing the parts of you that you have tended to distance yourself from in the past will instead take away the ability they have to hold you back.

NOTES

PART 2

DESIRED DESTINATION

Getting clarity around where you want to go

Now that you have assessed the traits, skills and experiences that you already possess, from the perspective of what you have rather than what you lack, it is time to lift your gaze to the horizon and see where you want to go. That said, I don't believe a precise final destination is necessary at this point. I say that because what you are going to do is identify a direction, and learn how your internal compass works so that you will always be able to check in to make sure you are on the right track.

To that end, this part of the book will cover values and goals.

It is common in the worlds of both business and personal development to talk about the importance of having clearly defined goals and committing to following through on them in order to achieve success. Personally, I believe more in setting a direction. That is certainly the approach that has served me best. Several times in my life I have set a general direction and started moving forward. Doing that requires qualities like decisiveness, commitment and readiness to take action, but it also leaves room for all the other great things that may be learnt and encountered along the way. I like being open to discovering things that I don't yet know that I don't know. The fact that I might have remained oblivious to these blind spots if I was on a mission towards a very specific goal is one of the reasons I prefer setting a direction. This approach leaves room for us to achieve something even better than we'd planned for.

I use a goal not as a destination, but as something that gets me going. I then take the next good step and the next good step, and as long as the steps I take are all deliberate and well thought out, I invariably find myself at a great destination. What I love about this method is that there is plenty of room for course correction along the way. One step is after all just one step, so if it turns out to be a step in the wrong direction it won't have taken me too far off course. On the other hand, if you've been working for months, or maybe years on the wrong goal and find yourself at a destination that looks nothing like what you wanted, you might wind up thinking that it's too much trouble to take corrective action because too much time and effort have already gone into the exercise of getting to your goal. You might decide to just live with the outcome you achieved even if it isn't right for you.

For now, I want you to know that you don't have to have one clearly defined goal in mind in order to start on a path toward meaningful change.

Chapter 5

VALUES

In this chapter, we're looking at values – what they are, where they come from, and why knowing yours is the key to living deliberately. Getting a handle on how values play out and shape who you are is fundamental to taking charge and changing your life's direction.

Knowing your values will help you understand the motivation behind the decisions you make in your personal and professional life. Once you understand what your values are, you can take advantage of the fact that values are like a compass that points towards your destination. Knowing you're on the right track because your compass is working properly will relieve stress, indecisiveness, and inner conflict. The great thing is that a decision you make based on your values will feel like the right decision for you even when there are conflicting interests at play. It is, however, important that you use *your* values as your compass rather than falling into the trap of using society's, your family's, or anyone else's values to make decisions.

Another point I want to make here is that determining who you want to be, and then acting in ways that align with that persona, is much more efficient than trying to figure out what you want to do and how to get there. When I say, 'whom you want to be', I don't mean for you to identify a role model you look up to. Instead, the objective is to identify the very best version of yourself. You will find that version somewhere in between who you are now and whom you aspire to be; it's the version of you that turns up when you are at your absolute best. This version reflects your values, and your values reflect what is important to you, both in yourself and in your life.

Even though they are affected by the experiences you have and influences around you, your values are rooted deep inside of you. They are the behaviours and traits most meaningful to you and reflect how you think, live and work. Whether you are aware of them or not, you have a core set of values that are determining how you feel about life. But if you were asked what your top three values are, I think there's a very good chance that you won't be able to bring them to mind. Or you might think that you know what your values are, and dismiss the question thinking that you don't need to delve into it. Either way, it will be useful to spend some time reviewing the way your life is going vis a vis your values.

One of the reasons you might not be aware of your values could be that you think everybody thinks/wants/likes the same things because they are somehow objectively right. That's because our values are part of the very fabric of who we are. If you think this sounds very similar to what was covered about strengths in Chapter 1 you are right. Strengths and values are very closely linked, so closely in fact, that values are sometimes called character strengths.

Just like your thoughts are constantly present in the form of a soundtrack playing in the background of your mind, so are your values ever present, and they play an important part in the quality of your life. That's why I want you to focus on the question of values so that you can make sure the values that are shaping your life are your own, and that they are up to date.

If you're wondering where your values have come from, it's simply a case of having picked them up through the interactions you've had with other people and experiences throughout your life. Essentially, they come from your community, your parents, your teachers, your religious leaders, and society as a whole. You are likely to have unconsciously adopted the values embedded in the community you were a part of during your formative years. That's why you probably think that how you feel about things is the same as how everybody else feels about them. You can have taken on your values because they just felt right to you, or for the very opposite reason. What I mean by that is that maybe you had an unpleasant experience with someone, and you wanted to make sure you didn't end up like that person, so you adopted values that were opposite to theirs. For example, maybe you didn't feel heard when you were growing up, so you adopted 'listening' as one of your values because you wanted to make sure you never put other people in the situation of 'not being heard'. Similarly, you might have rebelled against some of the values other people tried to push onto you because they didn't represent the kind of person you wanted to be.

Notwithstanding the fact that difficult and sad things happen in life, people who live in alignment with their values will normally feel that their life is quite 'right' for them. If that sounds like you, you'll be feeling satisfied, authentic, and confident in your ability to take setbacks in your stride most of the time. This is true whether you know what your values are or not, but as you now know, awareness is the launch pad for positive change because it enables you to have clarity, certainty and confidence moving forward.

This is why it is so helpful to identify our values. If you are reading this book because you just know that something needs to change but you're not quite sure what that is, or even why it needs to change, chances are that you are not living in alignment with your values. The result of this kind of misalignment is likely to manifest in feelings of being stuck, lost and dissatisfied. If on the other hand, you are someone who is facing inevitable change in the form of a restructuring of your professional or your personal life, I want you to start to control how you are feeling by defining your values. The time you spend on this will save you from going down the rabbit hole of fear and uncertainty that challenging circumstances like these have the potential to generate.

> **When we are not living in alignment with our values life can feel off-kilter.**

I would even go so far as to say that awareness of our values is a good starting point and foundation for success in general, and meaningful change in particular. I've been there, and I want you to know that if life has knocked you over, when you are down on your knees, staying true to your values will help you to get through to the other side. I say that because remaining grounded and in a state where we have access to a clear enough head to assess our options is infinitely easier if we know what our values are.

It's worth noting that sometimes the choices we are called on to make will be between different values. For example, do we take the kids to the beach on a Saturday and honour our value around Family, or do we volunteer another Saturday and honour our value around Community? Will we accept the offer of overtime again and honour our value around Financial Security, or have an evening off and honour our value around Balance?

Consciously knowing that either choice aligns with our values may alleviate some of the guilt we might otherwise feel about not prioritising the alternative value. Not only that, but when we become conscious of our values, and consciously use them to make choices like the ones above, it will be easier to manage the way we divide our precious time so that the same value doesn't miss out every time. In so doing, we can feel satisfied knowing that we can honour all of our values at different times.

Identifying your values

If you are not aware of what your values are right now, you could be living by the values set out by the society you have grown up in, and/or real or perceived expectations from other people. Consider this – if you value family time but work a 70-hour week in a demanding job, do you think you'll be free of stress and internal conflict? Would you feel differently about the same working week if your value was advancement? Meanwhile, if you value creativity and work in a strictly analytical role, your prospects of experiencing a high level of job satisfaction are reasonably poor. Similarly, if you value time more than money, but work in a role that pays you handsomely while demanding a lot more of your time than you'd like, your level of job satisfaction is likely to be equally poor.

In Chapter 3 we discussed the fact that the beliefs you are abiding by might be left over from earlier periods in your life when your needs and aspirations were quite different to what they are now. Similarly, if you are not aware of your values, the value set you're using to navigate your way through your life could have been handed down to you by others.

For some people, that works just fine, but for others there is an uncomfortable sense of dissonance in their life if these values have come to feel superficial, materialistic and/or uncomfortably restrictive. If this feels like the situation you are in, you might be chasing someone else's dream, and trying to live your life according to someone else's measure of success. This is the fast track to living a life lacking fulfilment.

The bottom line is that first identifying your values, and then living by them will lead to a greater sense of integrity, clarity and confidence, and a whole lot less stress.

EXERCISE

This exercise will help you gain clarity about what makes you tick. Discovering your values is not difficult, but it takes a little bit of time and reflection. Allow yourself some time to take notes on what comes up for you as you move through the points below.

- Start by thinking back on the times you were happiest in your personal and professional life. What was it that made you happy? Why did this make you happy?
- Think about the times you were most proud. What were you proud of?
- Then identify times you felt fulfilled and satisfied. What needs or desires were being satisfied?
- How did these experiences bring value to your life?

As you will start to see, focusing on things that light you up and make you feel good, rather than the things you don't want in your life, will set you on a path to becoming your absolute best. That's the person you want to be!

With the experiences you identified in the steps above in mind, download the values list I have provided for you here www.charlottehillenbrand.com.au/values Then circle the words that hold meaning for you, or simply read the list and write down your chosen words in the space at the end of this chapter.

There's nothing particularly scientific or exhaustive about a values list. It is simply a list of words representing things that people find inherently motivating. Each word is likely to hold similar yet different meanings to different people. That's ok, because we don't need any strict definitions here. We are only interested in the meaning the word has for you right now.

Working with a list of value words, as opposed to simply writing your own words down, can be quite advantageous because it might help you think more freely and identify angles you might have otherwise missed. There is no right or wrong way to do this though, so don't judge yourself as you follow the steps below.

- Circle up to 20 words on the values chart.
- Go over your chosen words again to see if you can group any similar values under one value word.
- Remove any values out of the original 20 that now seem less significant to you.
- By a process of elimination, decide on your top three values, and determine the order they sit in on the shortlist.

Each step of this process requires you to look deeper into yourself with complete honesty. The more honest you are with yourself, the more effective this exercise will be for you. Remember that you are not creating a wish list of words that you feel like you should live your life by. Even though your values will help you become the best, most authentic and fulfilled version of yourself, they still need to feel true in relation to who you are right here and now. It's worth noting that values are not created, they are discovered. I say that because as values are based deep inside of us, they were already there before you identified the 20 you wrote down a moment ago.

Now that you have a list of your three core values, I want you to think about them several times during the coming week, and consider whether they still feel right to you. Do they make you feel good about yourself? Would you be proud to share them with people that are important to you? Would you be able to stand by them even if they made you less popular? If at any stage you realise that they don't feel right in terms of who you are and whom you aspire to be, come back to your notes and your list of 20 values words and adjust it until you feel good about the values you've identified.

Then comes the most important part: assessing your life against these values. The whole point of knowing your values is, after all, to live a life that is fulfilling and satisfying. To this end, I want you to carefully consider these questions: Does your daily life (both on the personal and professional fronts) represent your values? Are your values reflected in the habits you have formed? If not, it's probably time to make some adjustments to the way you are living your life.

Of course, knowing your values is of no value unless you live by them. It's when you start using your values as your compass that they will bring you clarity, integrity, confidence, meaning, fulfilment and a genuine sense of being grounded and happy.

Using your values as your compass will bring you clarity.

I wonder if you've noticed that this exercise is all about *being*, not *doing*.

It would be easy to think that aligning your life with your values is difficult or time-consuming, but that's not the case. It's no more complicated than connecting the dots. You can do this by thinking, "How will doing X help me be more (of your core value)?" Or "How can I stay (true to your core value) while doing X?" When you start thinking this way, what you are doing is thinking about how you want to *be,* rather than what you want to *do.* Everything from the actions that you need to take, and the obligations you need to fulfil, will take on a new meaning when you start looking at them with reference to your values.

Interestingly, once you start looking at your daily life through your values filter, you will probably find over time that the things that don't align with your values tend to work themselves out of your life as you give them less focus.

As I mentioned earlier, values are based deep within us, and as such they tend to remain pretty stable from day to day and week to week. However, as we go through life our values are likely to change in line with the goals or the successes and milestones we achieve, along with the changes in circumstances we experience. Early on in your career, for example, things like competition, earning great money, and recognition might be important. After some years in the workforce, things like work-life balance, the quality of our relationships, and community involvement might become more important. What that means, among other things, is that it's worth revisiting this exercise from time to time.

Essentially, knowing our values is a lifelong exercise. I recommend that you make it part of your personal maintenance plan to do this exercise every three to five years, or whenever your circumstances change. It will also be helpful to revisit anytime your life starts to feel a bit unbalanced or off-kilter.

There are Values and then there is the question of Value

The type of values I have spoken about so far are the ones that are embedded in the very fabric of who we are. Whether we are aware of them or not, these values are at the core of that thing we call our life. They are the basis for our thoughts, actions, views and opinions. But even after we have found our values and learnt to use them to make choices and decisions, we can find ourselves feeling conflicted. That's because there are so many activities, causes and interests that compete for our attention and time, and that's why it can be helpful to think about what brings us value on a day-to-day basis. If finding your deeper values is a way to give you clarity, finding this day-to-day value is a way to give you energy.

Adding value to your everyday life will bring you energy.

The real gold here is found when you link things that bring value to your life to the activities you are already doing, or activities that you have to do on a day-to-day basis. I love this exercise because it's a win–win when you get to see the value everyday activities contribute to the quality of your life. This is especially true when it comes to tasks that you would not choose to do if you had the option of avoiding them. When you are able to see how even something tedious that someone else has assigned to you can add value to your week, you will have significantly reduced the amount of resistance you would otherwise feel.

I know that it can sometimes be difficult to find that link, but I promise it will be well worth it if you keep trying.

EXERCISE

This is an exercise to help you find or add value to your everyday life. Come up with three answers for each of the questions below, using the pages at the end of this chapter.

- What do you love to talk about?
- What do you love to think about?
- What information do you love to look up in books/documentaries/the internet/podcasts, etc?
- What skills would you like to learn?
- What do you already know a lot about?

Now ask yourself which of the three answers to each question inspires you the most, and why? Consider what feelings each of those answers brings up within you.

Next, consider whether you are including enough of them as you go about your week. If you recognise that some of the things you've identified are missing from your life, ponder why that is, and how you could redress this. Including pockets of something that lights you up or grabs your interest, even in a time-poor existence, can prove to be just the injection of energy you need to get all your to-do's done.

If you find this exercise a bit tricky, a technique that will make it easier for you to link the value to the task at hand, is to ask yourself "How can X (an activity you are already doing, or have to do) help you to experience more Y (one of your words from the list above that brings you value)?"

Here is an example from my family I'd like to share with you to make this a bit clearer. My daughter likes doing drama and knocks over anything she gets in the way of homework from her drama teacher without any difficulty. When it comes to chemistry, it's a different matter. As she finds chemistry more difficult and less fun than drama, she has to overcome resistance to getting down and doing her chemistry homework. Linking her drama and chemistry homework removes the resistance and adds value for her. It goes like this:

How can doing chemistry help you do more drama? That's easy! When you have done your chemistry work, you can do as much drama as you want! However, this is about more than just 'bribing yourself to do something difficult by promising the reward of doing something fun. Importantly, it works the other way too. When you reverse the question and link how doing something you want to do (drama) helps you do something you must do (chemistry), that's when you have deleted the resistance and instead added value. Keep linking the different activities in your thoughts, the ones you want to do and the ones you have to do, because as you have learnt a new neural pathway takes many repetitions to establish. It will soon become apparent that doing what you have to do will get you more of what you want.

This approach is powerful in many ways. Not only does it add value by enabling you to do both what you love, and what you have to do with relative ease. It also lets you start from a place of strength and jump into something you find difficult from that space of strength rather than resistance. It is like tackling an obstacle from above rather than trying to climb over it from below. I call it borrowing energy when we achieve something difficult by starting with something fun.

Here is how I added value by borrowing energy

I want to help you make sense of the point I made above by sharing an experience I had a number of years ago when I realised I needed an energy injection in my life. My daughters had reached an age where they no longer needed as much care as they used to, and I had reached the point in my professional life where it all felt very familiar and comfortable. I found myself in the enviable and comfortable situation of finally having not only my nose above the surface so to speak, but also having some spare capacity. The only problem with a situation like this is that being comfortable means that there could be room for doing more, as well as the converse proposition that recognises room for a degree of boredom to set in. The question for me was what *more* did I want? Was it time to apply for a new position at work now that I had some spare capacity to give to new tasks and responsibilities? I decided that it wasn't. I decided to enjoy the spare capacity by giving back to my family and myself, instead of investing it in stepping up a level or two in my career. However, it became obvious to me that an energy injection was required so that complacency and boredom wouldn't set in.

What I did to bring that about was apply a mental shift.

The mental shift involved deciding that I would switch the priority I was giving my work vis a vis the way I was treating my time off. Many of us, especially ambitious people who want to realise our full potential, tend to see work as the more important and 'serious' part of our life, and our time off is basically whatever is left over. I swapped that around and told myself that I was now going to see work as my hobby, and my time off as my main occupation. The result of this change in perspective was that when I packed my bag to go away for a few days of flying, I did it with a new level of energy and enthusiasm because after all, how lucky was I to be going away and enjoying my hobby undisturbed for four whole days. No one (including myself) would tell me I had more important things to do, so I could revel in my hobby, with the added bonus of staying in nice hotels with plenty of time to myself. What a great deal! Even though I had 'downgraded' work from being the most important activity in my life, both it and I benefitted in a big way from my mind shift. At the same time, whenever I had two or three days off at home, I had a renewed zeal when it came to making the time count by using it wisely to do meaningful things because this was my new main occupation. Among other things, I wanted to add creativity to my life, which was something that had been lacking in the highly technical and efficient world of a pilot that I had previously prioritised over my time off. I smile as I reflect on the fact that my art skills had stalled at the level of stick figures and mud maps in primary school, but they started developing again after I enrolled in drawing classes in an effort to make the most out of my spare time. I chose drawing rather than painting because I wanted something that would be easily accessible to me. That mattered because I knew myself well enough to know that I'd be more likely to follow through if I couldn't hide behind excuses like not having enough time to set up an easel, or painting being too messy and taking up too much space. Meanwhile, it was just too hard to argue that a sketch pad and a couple of pencils would be too much trouble to arrange. So, I took drawing classes and found immense joy in them. What's more, my sketches looked so much better than stick figures and mud maps in no time at all. It was a revelation to me that art was something that could be taught and learnt, not just an innate talent that special people are born with. Learning the new skill of drawing felt meaningful to me, and in the process, I found a great way to unwind and feel satisfied. But it didn't end there. I also started to think of everyday chores in creative terms. Instead of gritting my teeth over having to make dinner on a regular Tuesday night when the family was busy, tired and hungry, I reminded myself that I enjoy cooking and that it was more helpful to bring out that enjoyment on a Tuesday evening than save it for weekend dinners (which I was often not home for anyway). So, I recentred myself around this thought in a very deliberate way and was able to find both joy and meaning in the process. Looking for creativity in my everyday life, as well as looking at my everyday life creatively, made me more mindful and present. It was a beautiful thing because in a single stroke it made me both calmer and more energised. This simple mind shift, where I reprioritised the importance of my work life and my time off, was a win–win situation. Not only did I get to align the way I was living with my key values of Family, Creativity, and Curiosity, but it was incredibly easy. It cost nothing, it hurt no one and benefited everyone. I don't know how long I consciously kept thinking the thoughts that "This is now my hobby" and "This is now my main occupation." I guess the need to remind myself just became obsolete by the time my mind adjusted to this new normal that was so helpful on so many fronts. There was no need to go back to an old 'normal' once I had injected so much energy by having achieved so much more value in my everyday life.

Summary

Knowing our values is like having a compass; you can rely on them when you make decisions and choices. This will decrease second-guessing and guilt that can otherwise be present when different interests compete for your time and attention.

Taking some time to discover your values, and making sure they are current is a good way to start getting some clarity on what you want out of life.

When you live in alignment with your values your life will feel "right" even if it is still difficult. When you are out of alignment with your values your life will feel off-kilter and you will be experiencing more uncertainty and less clarity.

Knowing your values is a way to add clarity.

Doing activities that give you value on a day-to-day basis is a way to inject energy into your life. This can also mean seeing the value that doing the things you have to do will add to your life.

We can borrow energy from something we enjoy, to do the things we have to do but don't necessarily enjoy.

NOTES

NOTES

Chapter 6

A FEW THOUGHTS ON PURPOSE

One thing I struggled with in the aftermath of losing my flying career was finding my purpose, or rather coming to grips with whether I needed to find my purpose.

Experts in the field of positive psychology have concluded that a purpose is one of the main ingredients required to live a fulfilling life. To me, the word purpose sounds big and almost holy. I had been very happy for many years just flying people from A to B. Looking at the question of purpose prompted me to ask myself whether there was any deeper purpose to that, or if I had just been leading a meaningless, albeit very satisfying life.

I spoke to several people who shared that they too had felt some pressure around finding that one purpose above all others. Some of them noticed that they worried about not doing what they were supposed to do unless they could find their one purpose. After mulling it over I came to the conclusion that a purpose doesn't have to be huge. It just needs to be slightly bigger than we are. I also formed the conclusion that we don't have only one purpose. We can have purposes for different times in our life, and we can have purposes that satisfy different aspects of ourselves. I believe we get to choose, and importantly, we don't need to desperately search for that one elusive purpose.

When you know your strengths, you can craft your life in a way that enables you to use them as much as you can. And when you know your values and use them as a compass as you make choices and decisions, I feel that you will have turned yourself into the best version of yourself that you can be. In that state, I believe you will be able to contribute and find meaning in many different areas of your life. My firm belief is that wherever you can simultaneously contribute and find meaning, you will have purpose after all.

To sign off on this short chapter, I want to invite you to look at yourself, rather than what's around you, in order to find your purpose.

You will find your purpose in the best version of you.

NOTES

NOTES

Chapter 7

GOALS

A fundamental part of success is setting well-structured goals and doing what it takes to achieve them. Goal setting is a good habit to foster. Without goals, we don't have destinations to aim for during our trip through life. This is a problem for several reasons, not least of which is that without defining a destination, the only thing you can be sure of is that you will never get there.

But how do you set an effective goal you might be wondering. Is it best to have an easily achievable goal, or should you set goals that are slightly out of your reach in order to extend your capacity? Should you set a big life goal or many small goals, and when should you set and revise your goals?

Let's look at the question of goals from different angles.

Are SMART goals smart?

A well-known and much-used goal-setting model is called SMART goals. SMART is an acronym for the words Specific, Measurable, Attainable, Relevant and Time-based. A goal with those five ingredients in it is quite concrete and therefore easier to take action on than less-defined alternatives. It also allows us to easily know when the goal has been completed. It works well for short-term or interim goals in particular because it provides consistent affirmation around whether we are accomplishing things and moving forward.

But let's look at these types of specific goals with a wider perspective.

Let's say you have always dreamt of working in a specific position in a specific company or for a specific person. You've made that your goal and you throw everything at it. You do whatever you can, sacrifice a lot, and don't just give it your best shot, you give it your all.

That kind of determination, dedication, and perseverance is unquestionably commendable. I am sure that if that's how you operate you are a person with a high degree of discipline, and other excellent habits that will serve you well. But if your goal is that specific it is also likely to be very fragile because if it is only one specific position you are vying for, the truth is that you only have one single chance at reaching your goal.

A very specific goal is also very fragile.

That said, it is certainly possible for you to achieve that goal even if it is just one position, because you might well be the right person for it. Don't ever think you can't throw your hat in the ring because there are going to be hundreds of candidates vying for just one position. Switch your thinking to focus on the fact that you only need one position, and there is no need for you to worry about the other candidates' suitability.

Notwithstanding what we just covered in the paragraph above, let's consider the question of what will happen if you don't get the job. It's worth fleshing this out because whether you are aware of it or not, this is one of the doubts that's likely to be playing in the back of your mind. Possibly you've been preparing yourself for this goal for years. You've given it your all, and someone else gets the job over you. Do you feel like you failed? There are several ways you can look at a scenario like this. Having failed is certainly one of them. We'll come back to this soon, but let's start by looking at how you set your goal before we go there.

When did you set your goal?

This specific career goal of yours might have been seeded when you were in your teens. Maybe it was during high school when you were choosing subjects based on their ability to get you into the right course at university to get the degree you need to apply for the job you're striving for now. If that's the case, it's worth asking yourself whether it is still a valid choice, or whether it's time to reflect on how well the job in question suits the person you are now.

Whose goal is it?

Time and time again we hear about people who realise somewhere along the track that they are following someone else's dream. Something wakes them up to an awareness that the goal they are working towards is set up by real or perceived expectations from an external source. Similarly, it's not uncommon for people to realise that they are measuring their success against someone else's scale. This might be the case if something is irking you at the moment, and you don't quite know what it is.

Being clear on whether your goal is still valid, and whether it is really yours is essential. So is knowing what success looks like to you. If there's ever any doubt about this, referring back to your values will help you to work out what's going on, and to sort your priorities out. For example, if time and freedom are more important to you than money, you should allow yourself to feel successful when you have set your life up in a way that provides you with an optimal amount of spare time at your disposal.

Widen your goal

It can be helpful to make your goal quite broad from the outset. It can still include some very specific aspects, but broadening it lets you open your mind to making the most of any opportunities you encounter along the way. You might even stumble on an opening you could never have dreamt of before you heard about it. This is because we don't know what we don't know, so setting a very specific goal early on could prove to be rather limiting.

I also want to urge you to be open to changing your goal along the way if needs be. This is not a cop-out or a sign that you're not committed enough. Staying true to your original goal is terrific as long as it doesn't blind you to other opportunities along the way. Little is gained if you reach your goal but miss out on maximising your potential. Making your goal broad not only increases your chances of achieving it, but it also leaves room for the possibilities that could emerge if you don't have blinkers on in the way of a tightly defined goal.

> *There is no point in reaching your goal but missing out on your potential.*

My personal favourite is to end a goal with "… or better". That kind of goal setting removes any limitations while letting you maintain a level of specificity that is going to keep you focused.

Goal vs process

As you can see now, there are ways to set goals other than just making them SMART. Like I said at the beginning of part two, for my own part, I believe setting a general direction works best for me. It feeds my curiosity, and my curiosity drives forward momentum. This approach allows me to tap into my intuition, which is a skill anyone can develop. The great thing about intuition is that like our muscles, it becomes stronger and more accurate the more we use it.

Not everyone is like that though, and you might find it easier to get into action and create forward momentum if you have something more specific than a general direction. This is where setting a short-term SMART goal can be truly helpful to get you moving. My twist on setting a SMART goal is to not be too attached to it. Allow yourself to grow out of your goal. I say that because I've seen people set goals that they eclipse when they realise what they are capable of and what else is possible. In these instances, goal setting was just something that got the process started. The bottom line is that I don't want you to be stymied by the approach you take to setting your goals.

A goal can be a starting point rather than an endpoint.

Whether to stick to your goal – or not

The first thing I want to say here is that there's no point in thinking you've failed if you don't reach a goal that was possibly not even right for you in the first place. I also want you to remember that changing track in terms of your goals is not the same thing as giving up. You can use your goal as a stepping stone or even a springboard that propels you forward. It could turn out to be the case that leaving your goal behind for something else is the thing that gets you ahead. Giving up, on the other hand, only sets you back.

There is, however, also the matter of having to stick to your goal long enough so that you can properly evaluate whether it is right for you and whether or not you are making progress.

It is not always easy to identify which of these circumstances you are in. Is it a matter of having outgrown your goal, or are you wanting to give up because it feels too hard, or have you not done enough yet to even be able to evaluate your options properly? Considering previous experiences, tapping into your gut feeling, and taking time to reflect will help you to get clarity.

> **Not reaching a goal that wasn't right in the first place is no failure.**

Summary

Once we know our values we can embed them in the compass we use when we're making decisions. Having this kind of foundation in place makes the business of decision-making easier because it does away with inner conflict, uncertainty, and guilt.

You will feel more aligned once you know and start living by your values. It will bring you more ease, joy and energy.

Making the connection between the things that you value and the things you already do will inject even more energy and ease into your life.

Consider your goals carefully and make sure they are current and yours.

Set your goals in a way that is specific enough to motivate you to take action, and as wide as you can make them to allow for any unknown opportunities that emerge.

Use goal setting as a way to start a process of change, and never be afraid of leaving a goal behind if you outgrow it.

NOTES

NOTES

PART 3

TAKE OFF

Doing things differently

So far you have been setting the foundations for the new transformed version of yourself to emerge. It is my hope that after working your way through Parts 1 and 2 of this book you are looking at yourself a bit differently than you were before. I hope you have allowed yourself to see all that you are, all that you have accomplished, and all that you have to offer. I also hope you can see that you have accomplished these things because you are who you are: it is your thoughts, choices, decisions and the ways you have executed everything you are finding out about yourself that is reflected back to you in the comprehensive asset list you came up with.

Remember that your asset list also included the parts of you that you might not have been proud of in the past. Perhaps you were ashamed to 'own' these parts of yourself. Bringing them into the light and owning them has enabled you to watch them pale in comparison to all of the assets you identified. This might be the first time you've embraced all that you are, and I hope that you can recognise that there is room for it all and more. In fact, there is not only room for it all, but there is a need for it all. I say that because you can only be your best when you also accept your worst.

In Part 2 we focussed on getting clear about your desired destination. This matters because without a destination you have no way of knowing if you are on the right track or not. However, I also suggested that a general direction might be sufficient to start you off. When I worked as a pilot we only ever diverted for negative reasons, when something prevented us from continuing to our destination. In life, I want to make room for deviations for all sorts of positive reasons instead. Broadened horizons, new perspectives, new skills, insights and awareness are all positive reasons for you to choose a different destination. This last section of the book is all about how to take action. You will find several ways to add a new perspective to what you are doing in the following chapters. These are not delivered in the form of a list of action steps that you follow from beginning to end, but rather suggestions around how you can look at things differently. Needless to say, some will resonate with you more than others, and different suggestions are likely to feel more suited to different situations or different times than others. My hope is that you'll find something helpful for each moment, especially if you're feeling demotivated or stuck in some way.

There are no exercises as such in this last part of the book. Instead, it is up to you to try the different perspectives I present whenever you need to take action.

Chapter 8

TAKE ACTION – FROM A DIFFERENT PERSPECTIVE

In order to achieve a different outcome, you need to do something differently or turn your focus to different things. Albert Einstein is credited with the phrase – "Insanity is doing the same thing over and over and expecting a different result."

Looking at things differently is a good first step when you are wanting to do things differently in order to create change in your life. This is because when we change the way we look at things, the things we look at change. We already touched upon this when we talked about what your brain filters into your consciousness.

If you have allowed yourself to reflect on your situation while working your way through this book, you might have noticed a shift in your perspective already. This could be the result of a change in your mindset or an enhanced level of awareness around your thoughts. To get the benefits from these things you need to put your new insights into action.

This matters because thinking and acting differently about the life you've been living can create massive change in the trajectory of your life. That might be the only change you need. You might have been thinking that what you were needing was a new job or home or partner, or something of that magnitude, only to find that a different perspective opens the way to creating positive change within your existing arrangements. That's why this internal work is so important. It gives you agency to see all the things that you can in fact control.

In case there was a niggling doubt in the back of your mind, I hope you can see that all of the self-reflection and introspection you have done so far was not in the interest of self-indulgence.

Much like being told to put the oxygen mask on yourself before helping other people when there's a drop in pressure on a flight, creating lasting and rewarding change in your life is best done by focusing on yourself first and then putting that best version of you in life's way. It's that best version of you that is now going to adopt some new perspectives on how you do and see things. It might seem like a shortcut to you to go straight into this chapter and start with the actionable suggestions I offer here. However, just like so much else in life, you will find that laying a good foundation first will prove to be the quickest and easiest way in the end. So too, doing the inner work first and then applying these new perspectives will prove to be the fastest and most stable way to sustainable change.

Act from a different perspective

You take yourself with you wherever you go.

That is an indisputable fact. You can change the circumstances around you all you want, but if you keep thinking and acting the same way you always have there's next to no chance that you'll find yourself in a substantially better position. If you want things to be different, you need to do something differently; it's as simple (and as difficult) as that.

We are the sum of all the choices and decisions we make. We cannot keep making choices that don't align with the life we want to be living, with the view to making other choices once we 'get there', because we will simply never get there in the first place if we approach things that way. Just like we will never be able to squeeze apple juice out of an orange, we will never be able to create the life we want from doing the things we've been doing that sustain the life we (for one reason or another) don't want.

Therefore, now that it is time to take action to craft the life you want to be living, I suggest you do it from a different perspective than the one that got you to where you are now. I share some of the different perspectives that have been very helpful to me in this chapter. While it doesn't lay out a step-by-step process for you to follow, it offers you different perspectives that can help you move forward in a new way. I suggest you try some of them out and notice what works for you. Keep using the ones that give you the kinds of results you're after and discard the ones that don't, but don't dismiss any without trying them. Please notice that I say, 'try them'. I want to stress that, because no matter how effective these tools have been for others, they'll have zero chance of working for you if you don't use them.

—

Do things differently in order to get a different result.

—

Act like your new identity

When we spoke about values earlier, I explained that you will find yourself somewhere between where you are now and where you aspire to be.

When you take action in line with your new direction and are guided by your values, it is very useful to leverage the qualities of the person you aspire to be and act as if you are that person already. Seeing yourself as someone who has already achieved what you want to achieve lets you make your decisions from a different place. This will help you gain momentum and stay on track.

The very first thing I asked you to do in this book was to picture yourself as a vital and successful 70-year-old, looking back over your amazing life. The reason I wanted you to do this was to embed the idea of you being a successful person by feeling what that would be like. The simple act of thinking of yourself as having achieved all the things you want to achieve is more powerful than you might think. So, to start using that persona as your guide, and to tap into the motivation a guide like that can provide, I want you to consider what you did to get to that moment in your life. Who were you? What decisions and choices did you make? This exercise highlights the obvious (but often overlooked) truth of the fact that your life is the sum of your choices.

On a concrete day-to-day basis, this means you should take the action a person getting the results you want to get would take. Identifying yourself and your behaviour with the results you want can help a lot when you are uncertain of what the next step is, when you are tempted to procrastinate, or when you just feel stuck.

Things like a lack of time, doubt, and procrastination sometimes turned up for me while I was in the process of writing this book. I would get myself back on track tapping away on my laptop by asking myself the question, "What would an author do?" That's an easy one to answer – sit down and write of course! This kept me motivated and clear about what to focus on.

Acting like your new identity can be a useful strategy for any part of your life: What would a healthy person choose to eat? What would a runner do? What would a person who regularly aces their exams do? Asking questions like these can cut out a lot of procrastination and indecisiveness. What's more, once you start doing something, the next thing becomes easier to do. Very soon you will notice that when you make your decisions from a different space to the one where your results were patchy at best, your decisions and their results will start adding up to a new life for you.

Make your decisions as if you already are the person you want to become.

Long-term view

When you identify yourself as a certain kind of person, as per the section above, not only are you making your decisions from a different space. You are also making a long-term commitment to being that person. It has been proven that this approach in itself is a catalyst for learning and change. A study from the University of Melbourne (1997) showed that a long-term commitment even when combined with less practice, accomplished faster improvement in music students than a short-term commitment combined with more training. It was the long-term perspective and identification with the outcome that made these music students excel, even though they had less practice under their belt than the others.

> Adopt a long-term view to
> fast-track your learning.

Mental rehearsal

Mental rehearsal is a technique that has been used successfully by top athletes for many years. You might have heard it called visualisation. The term mental rehearsal more accurately describes what I'm talking about here, and allows for a wider scope in terms of what you can include in your rehearsal. Brain scans show that the parts of the brain activated by action are the same parts of the brain activated by simply thinking vividly about an action. As far as your brain is concerned, they are the same!

Studies have shown that test subjects were able to build muscle mass by simply imagining they were doing an exercise program, while other test subjects gained improvement in their piano playing skills by imagining they were practising playing the piano.

I find these studies utterly fascinating, but they don't surprise me. I say that because mental rehearsing is something all pilots do throughout their careers. You've probably seen (even if only in movies) the flight deck of a modern airliner, with all its buttons, switches and levers. It is not possible to learn it all while sitting in the actual flight deck because aircraft like that don't spend much time on the ground. Even time in flight simulators is limited, so we start learning in front of a paper cockpit, or even a poster on the wall at home. This is how we not only learn where things are but also program our muscle memory so that our hands can locate each switch without necessarily having to be looking at it. By the time we start training in the flight simulator, our hands already know where to go.

Mental training, or dry flying as we call it, is something pilots do continuously. Every time I stepped into my hotel room for the night, I mentally rehearsed the actions required in case of an engine failure after take-off, and when I went for a run, I'd mentally go through even longer scenarios. This is how pilots are able to stay current and prepared for events that might never actually happen to them.

Mental rehearsal can be used for any situation. You can mentally rehearse drills, conversations, scenarios and more. It is most effective when you include all of your senses, and imagine yourself doing what you need to do as vividly as possible. Don't see it like a movie where you view yourself doing these things, but be in yourself as if you are already doing it. Mentally go through the motions in as much detail as you need, and add your other senses: what are you seeing? What are you hearing? Can you smell anything? Is there a breeze against your skin? First, rehearse what you need to do as if you are successfully doing it, and then add the aftermath which might be a big smile on your face after you have accomplished the task at hand, or people cheering and congratulating you for a job well done – whatever it looks like and will resonate with you.

By rehearsing like this, as vividly as you can, you might also discover where possible stumbling blocks will be. Is part of the task particularly difficult? Is something making you particularly nervous about it? Your mental rehearsal can alert you to problem areas and enable you to come up with a plan to handle them in advance. Some aspects of the task in question might need more actual preparation. For example, you might need to mentally rehearse your strategy for dealing with different emotions or overcoming particularly difficult obstacles.

That said, make sure the scenario you rehearse most frequently is the one where you succeed effortlessly.

> **Rehearse mentally in order to make faster progress.**

The power of small steps

As a high achiever you are used to getting things done and you're not scared of a challenge. Large amounts of work, important work, difficult work, long hours – none of that phases you because you are competent and self-sufficient. The only problem is that it's easy to fall into the trap of an all-or-nothing mindset when you operate like that. In this context, I want to introduce you to the power of the small step - that step that is so small you might think it isn't even worthwhile. Let me explain why it is indeed worthwhile to take that step.

From time to time, you might come up against a situation that feels just a bit too unfamiliar or too big, and you might feel stunned, or not able to take action because what is in front of you is simply too much for you to take on at the moment.

A small step is all it will take to get you moving. Break down your task into smaller and smaller parts, until you get to an action that is small enough to make getting started feel easy. Getting started is the crucial thing here. This strategy is about moving away from the all-or-nothing mindset to an all-or-something mindset. When you have taken that ridiculously small first step, the second one will feel easier to take, and then the third ... So instead of getting stuck in excuses to justify why you can't take on that big project – "I don't have time," "I don't have the money," "It is too difficult" – you can get yourself in motion by taking one small step, and then let momentum do most of the work moving forward.

Imagine two ladders next to each other. One ladder has rungs that are close together and easy to climb. The other ladder has wider spaces between the rungs. Fewer steps are required to reach the top of this ladder, but each step is more difficult than it is on the ladder with the closer rungs. Even though having fewer, but more difficult steps might look tempting, you will not get anywhere if you spend your time fretting over how to reach that first step. Meanwhile, you can watch the person on the ladder next to yours take their small easy steps and reach the top of the ladder quickly and effortlessly. A small step can also mean a short time. For tasks that you don't enjoy doing but nevertheless need to do, setting a timer for 15 minutes can lessen the emotional drag and potential for procrastination. Who can't do a boring or uncomfortable task for 15 minutes? If after those 15 minutes you've had enough, or you have other things to do, put the boring task away and give yourself a pat on the back for the 15 minutes of work on it that you did do. While you are at it, notice the amount of work you were able to accomplish in that short time when you knew you weren't bound to spend the rest of the day on the boring task. You might be amazed at how much can be accomplished in such a short time. You might even find that when the timer goes off you are so deeply into the task that you don't want to stop, so by all means keep going and again congratulate yourself for breaking through the mental barrier you had and achieving much more than you had expected. The 15-minute trick is useful for anything from writing a book to sorting through emails, to doing a tidy-up around the house. Taking small steps is not just a great way to get started. It is also a great way to stay on track on those days when your energy is low, or for some other reason, you're simply unable to perform at your best. We all have days like that. Asking yourself, "What's the least I can do?" will keep you moving forward even when you think you can't do anything. Having 'the next smallest step' as your eternal backup plan will let you slip up, or rest, even as you keep progressing.

How I have used small steps

My fitness was completely shot after having shingles several years ago. I have always been active and fit, and suddenly I was just tired and worn out all the time. A couple of years previously I had returned to running. It was something I enjoyed when I was younger, and I was proud to have gotten my fitness up to a level where I had ran a half marathon. Several months after being sick I couldn't even imagine running for 10 minutes. I shared my frustration with a friend who is a personal trainer. What she said was, "Don't even think about running 10 minutes. Just go for a walk, and run for one minute during that walk. After a few days run one and a half minutes during the same walk. That's how you build up your fitness slowly." Running for one minute sounded ridiculous to the ears of someone who had recently done a 21km half marathon, but that's what I did. I started running for one minute, and eventually I got my fitness back on track and I ran my second half marathon.

Even after this experience, I had to remind myself of the power of small steps when I found myself in the same position after having covid. I went back to one-minute runs because I knew from first-hand experience that this approach would get my fitness back up to where I wanted it a lot quicker than fretting over not being able to run for 10 minutes.

What is the smallest step you can take right now to keep moving forward?

Allow yourself to be a beginner

Letting yourself be a beginner when you are learning something new is a great way to get to where you want to be. Somehow, we seem to think that adding years to our life, and the experiences we encounter is all it will take to be competent all-round. It doesn't work that way though. No one has knowledge and skills without learning them, because what's new to us is new to us – end of story.

Not only do you need a growth mindset so you can see that it's possible to learn new things, but you also maximise your chances for success when you allow yourself to be a beginner. You will cut time and effort when you accept that you are a beginner and seek instruction from a teacher or coach. The truth is that figuring things out is not the same thing as learning.

From where I sit it's clear that thinking we should already be proficient at new things is silly and – may I add, it's somewhat vain to think that we are so smart that we don't have to learn new things. Just like the person climbing the ladder quicker by taking smaller steps, accepting that you are a beginner will position you to overtake the person who is too headstrong to take up the opportunity to learn properly by starting from the beginning and getting the help they need. Maybe on the other hand though, you're like me and find it enormously empowering and humbling to be an adult beginner.

Allow yourself to be a beginner, and you will progress faster.

Redefine failure

Thomas Edison, the man who invented the light bulb, is known to have said, "I haven't failed. I have discovered 10,000 ways that don't work." And Nelson Mandela said, "I don't fail. I either succeed or learn". Needless to say, both Mandela and Edison had growth mindsets. I think it's fair to say that they didn't allow setbacks to hold them back. There are innumerable other examples of successful people saying similar things as these two great men, because the fact is that for any innovation to be possible, we have to allow ourselves to see failure as a natural part of learning. To this end, many companies have failure built into their business model, and employees are instructed or encouraged to fail quickly. This is an effective way to make the idea of failure non-threatening, and it's a great way of building a thriving culture around exploring, learning and innovation. I applaud that because where the discomfort of failure leads to a culture of fear, blame and shame, learning opportunities are in short supply. The word 'failure' belongs in a place where minds are fixed and narrow, opportunities are limited, things are either/or, and the time perspective is very short. In this place, you either can or can't, and you either win or lose. But if instead, we redefine failure to mean lessons, there is room and time to grow. Accepting failure is a good start but it doesn't account for the fact that the word itself is loaded with negativity. However, when we redefine failure as a learning opportunity, we don't have to take the detour into the ditch where our ego gets hurt, blame and excuses abound, and we have to dig deep and coax ourselves to have another go. So why not leave the concept of failure out completely? I've had my fair share of failures, and I haven't liked them one little bit. They hurt because they made me feel small and incompetent and made me doubt myself. My failures have happened, as they tend to do, when I was already feeling weak for some reason or other.

One story of failure

Every airline pilot has to undergo regular simulator training and checking of their competency several times a year. These are rather gruelling sessions. They entail four hours of very intense hard work in the simulator book-ended by briefing sessions before and after the time spent in the simulator. All up, the sessions take almost eight hours. During a simulator session, we train for different scenarios including all types of technical failures and emergencies of other kinds.

These sessions were challenging (mentally and sometimes physically), especially when they were scheduled in the middle of the night. It is a pass-or-fail arrangement, where if you fail you are 'out of service' until you have done another check and passed, so the stakes are high. The last two hours of the second night of simulator work were when I would be checked. By that time, I was tired, not just from working two consecutive night shifts, but from the fact that those two night shifts were by far the most challenging experiences we had in our whole roster.

Don't worry, I completely agree that pilots should be checked on their ability to handle difficult conditions. I completely get that anything can happen at any time and a pilot needs to be prepared for anything even at 2 am, but this doesn't take away from the fact that it was hard work. At 2 am on the second night, when both my colleague and I were drained after having worked harder than we had in the previous six months combined, was when I had to perform at my very best. The pressure was on, and the stakes were high. And I failed on a couple of occasions. I stumbled out of the simulator with my tail between my legs feeling embarrassed, depleted and defeated. Not to mention small and insignificant, and seriously questioning myself about whether I had what it took.

In hindsight, I could see that the lead-up to the sessions I failed had something in common in terms of the attitude I went into them with. You see, from time to time I would get fed up with constantly being checked. It felt like I was being poked and prodded, and always being supervised like a little girl who never got to grow up. I don't know of any other profession that is monitored as much as piloting. It was not only the regular checks when we were being scrutinised; every day everything a pilot does or doesn't do is monitored and recorded.

Every pilot that I know feels a level of stress in the lead-up to sim which is what we 'affectionately' call these mandatory challenges. There were a number of pilot dads at my children's school. Sometimes I would sit outside the classroom at pickup time talking to the other mums waiting for their children, and I might say I was busy studying for sim. The other pilots' wives in the group would say, "I hate sim! I just want to close the door to my husband's study when he is preparing for sim and not let him out until it's done, because he is just so grumpy." They hated sim, the spouses! Interacting with these women gave me a sense that the stress I felt around sim was normal and justified.

Looking back on it now, it's clear that feeling the stress, and being fed up with being 'poked and prodded' was not a good mindset to be in for learning and performing well. I was stuck in a fixed mindset, where we think we either have what it takes or we don't, and there is not much we can do about it. Or we may feel entitled and therefore see it as unjust that we should have to submit ourselves to being tested. You'll remember from the mindset chapter that I filled you in on the way having everyone around me thinking it was so special that I was a pilot sometimes nudged me into having a fixed mindset in that part of my life. Even though I didn't know much about mindset at the time, I still knew that more generally I was a curious person who was eager to learn. It's interesting to note the difference between the attitude I adopted in the context of preparing for simulator checks when I was a bit off and inclined to be in a fixed mindset, compared to the more positive attitude I displayed when I reminded myself that I am a curious person who likes to learn. I would tell myself things like "How lucky am I to have a learning opportunity like sim in front of me?" "Studying is easy for me." "I happily take up every opportunity to learn." I used these phrases like mantras that primed me to do well during my preparation for sim.

Those times were the ones where I approached the simulator sessions with a lot more ease. I even told myself I was looking forward to it. I was able to see that it was just one of those things that I had to do, and as I already had the skills required, it was just another day at work for me, really. You won't be surprised to hear that not only was the outcome better, but the road there was so much less stressful. That's what a growth mindset does for us. It leaves us room to grow. When we give ourselves room to grow there is always an upside.

Think of it as learning instead of failure, and keep learning until you succeed.

Taking responsibility

Life changed for me the day I realised that taking responsibility for all my actions and reactions made things easier, not harder. Among other things, taking full responsibility gave me more agency, and things that I had considered difficult became easier. What's more, I was no longer bothered or annoyed by others. The perspective shift that came with my taking responsibility totally changed how I saw things that I had previously perceived as failure or rejection.

One of our human traits is to blame others. It's a seemingly easy way out when we feel we have done our part and things still don't go our way, and it surely has to be someone or something else at fault. Thinking this way both protects and nurses our ego, and it leaves us with a sense that our work was done, and the rest was up to someone else who didn't deliver. That someone else can be anyone – your boss, your partner, the person in the other car, our government, or more broadly 'the system'.

What we don't realise is that the downside of blame is that we disempower ourselves when we make our happiness or the positive outcome of our efforts dependent on someone or something else beyond our control. And as we can never control the reactions of other people, we render ourselves the victim of their whims and the conditions they set up. The reality is though, that if we are waiting for someone else to act or react in a certain way before we can be happy, we might be waiting for a very long time. What seemed easy at first – blaming someone else – has instead seen us unconsciously give away our power.

By taking responsibility you take back your power. When you can see that your problems (perceived or real), are yours to solve, it will free you up to take any necessary action, and you will see the attitudes and actions of people around you shift. Taking responsibility puts you in the driver's seat. You can now choose your course of action, rather than wait for others to say or do the things you expect and need them to do. In the end, taking responsibility will prove to be the easier, most direct way to achieve what you're striving for after all.

This is not at all the same thing as taking responsibility for other people's actions or mistakes. Neither is it an excuse to make yourself a martyr and think, "The only way to get anything done the right way is to do it myself." That is just another way of blaming others. The act of taking responsibility is the very opposite of this. You decide to do the next right thing because it is the right thing to do. You don't need to wait for people around you to be in the right mood. When you step into the power of taking responsibility for your actions and your outcomes, using excuses is no longer an option because you can see it as the waste of time it is.

―

Taking responsibility for your actions, and inactions, puts you in the driver's seat.

―

Get past impossibilities by adding uncertainty

When you are very stuck, adding some uncertainty into the mix can help unstick the situation. You didn't misread that, and it is not a typo. It might seem contradictory, but let me explain.

When you have a very fixed idea about something you want to achieve, you are only able to see very limited solutions for achieving it. The more certain you are about a situation that someone else has a different view of, the more stuck you will feel and the harder it will be to resolve the situation. If you are able to see it from a different perspective though, hence adding a degree of uncertainty to your own very certain standpoint, the stalemate loosens enough for other possibilities to enter the arena. That's when it's possible to say, "I can see that there are different ways to look at this," while at the same time not completely capitulating or giving up. It might sound like a noble thing to do, but it is also a strategy that will serve you well. Whether you are stuck in some kind of conflict with another person or stuck in circumstances that you feel you have no control over, thinking "How else can I look at this" opens up the opportunity to find a new more helpful perspective. This will let you find solutions you didn't previously consider.

Seeing a different perspective can help you get unstuck.

Consider best-case scenarios

In our deficit focussed culture, where we put more effort into noticing weaknesses than strengths, and where the negativity bias predisposes us to focus more on and respond more strongly to negative input than positive, we are used to letting our minds go straight to worse case scenarios. When we do that, we are not thinking of factual scenarios or even likely scenarios. Instead, we are thinking of possible scenarios. The fact is that positive scenarios are also possible, even if you deem them as less likely. And no matter what's going on at any given time, positive thoughts are equally available to you as negative ones are.

This example illustrates this well. If you get wind of the fact that your supervisor wants to talk to you, do you think, "What have I done wrong?" or do you think, "I wonder what the good news is?" Each of these thoughts is equally available to you, and at this stage, you have no idea what your supervisor wants. For all you know she might just want to ask if you can recommend a great restaurant. So why not consider possible positive reasons, or at least neutral ones, rather than worst-case scenarios? Entering your supervisor's office with an expectation of hearing something positive, or at least if it's somewhat less than positive knowing that no harm is intended, will alter the way you show up. By not being defensive or on your guard you change the energy of the situation and take the stress out of what could otherwise have become quite tense. In so doing, you have done your part in setting the scene for an open unbiased and non-confrontational interaction.

Allow yourself to consider best-case scenarios.

Think that it's easy

Think "This is easy" even when the thing you're facing is challenging or downright difficult.

Telling yourself it's easy turns on a different switch in your brain and makes way for solutions to appear.

Keep a have-done-it-list

Most people have a to-do list that they never get to the end of. Either the day isn't long enough to get completion on anything, or they are constantly adding things to the list so that they never get anywhere near a clean slate. Operating like this is likely to make you feel stressed and inadequate. The list which was meant to help you has instead become a burden, reminding you of your shortcomings.

Here is my suggestion: keep a have-done-it-list. This involves writing the tasks you've completed on your have-done-it-list. I prefer this approach because, at the end of the day, you will have a list that highlights your accomplishments instead of your shortcomings. This is a simple approach to experiencing a sense of achievement, which will help you maintain momentum, and act from a place of strength rather than deficit or weakness. It's still helpful to transfer any important items for tomorrow onto a new shortlist. The difference is that you will be able to approach this with less dread when you can leverage the momentum you've gathered with this gentle yet profound shift in perspective focussed on noticing what you have achieved, rather than what you haven't.

Keep a have-done-it-list to see and acknowledge your progress.

Some thoughts on positive thinking

Too positive?

The focus of this book is about turning your attention from weakness to strength, from can't to can, and from limitations to possibilities. This is not to say that it is about turning negatives into positives or wrongs into rights. Instead, it's a more subtle mission I'm wanting to take you on to find a helpful approach. Only you can decide what that is for you.

Even though I prefer not to use the words positive or negative if I can help it, I don't deny that a shift towards what can be generalised as positive rather than negative is helpful for most people. For ease of reading, I will use the words positive and negative in this section to clarify my points, but there is a nuance to the way I'm using these words because they can both in their own way be limiting. And as a wise person once said to me, "Words are funny – we think they mean something."

I like to think of it along a scale with zero in the middle and negative numbers on one side, and positive ones on the other. You'll be aware that much of this book so far has been about raising your awareness around things that are on the negative side of the scale. These are things like your brain wanting to keep you safe by resisting exposing you to things that are new and unknown. This fear is further fuelled by the negativity bias that makes us notice and remember unpleasant experiences twice as much as pleasant ones.

As you're aware now, our unconscious thoughts and beliefs may not serve us as well as they could, and remember that our brain's filters give us more of what we already focus on. This may result in even more negative thoughts and experiences. Summarised like this, you'll see that there are a lot of things that pile up on the negative side of the scale. So, when I ask you to focus on your strengths and the positive experiences in your life, it is not to promote what some people call toxic positivity. Instead, by becoming aware of the negative tilt that seems to be the norm, you may catch it and turn it around.

As you have just seen above, there is probably room for a lot of positive reframes simply to outweigh the negatives your brain and your mind are subconsciously creating for you. Don't be afraid that you will become a practitioner of toxic positivity. Just give yourself a chance to get on an even footing with your negative self.

Piggyback on positive thoughts

You now know that your thoughts can be looked at as actual physical events because they are electrochemical signals in your brain that alter the physical landscape inside your body. They do this by way of the physical responses they elicit, for example through the release of hormones like dopamine and adrenaline.

You also know that you are the only thinker in your head, and that positive thoughts are just as available to you as negative ones. What's more, you know that positive thoughts are available to you even when the circumstances around you are not particularly positive. This is not the same thing as turning something negative into something positive or even looking for the positive in the negative. Instead, finding positive thoughts about anything will help you in a negative situation because it will activate your body's feel-good system. It is not about thinking happy thoughts about what you find unpleasant, it is about finding helpful thoughts to focus on instead of what you find unpleasant.

What I'm getting at here is that you can piggyback your way out of a negative situation by finding both peace and energy from positive thoughts. You can also use this approach when preparing for something you find difficult. Set yourself up by thinking of something you find easy or pleasant, and the energy boost this gives you is like tackling the obstacle from above rather than climbing over it from below.

Positivity vs Equanimity

After so many mentions of positive thinking, I want to return to my fundamental approach around the fact that it is not really about being positive, it is about finding perspectives and habits that are helpful. My view is that even though adding positive thinking can help get you out of negativity, aiming for equanimity is more helpful in the long term.

Equanimity is a restful state. I believe it is also a very resilient state. Like the tennis player returning to the baseline so that they will be prepared for any shot, being in a state of equanimity positions you well to respond to whatever happens around you because (among other things) it is a space where your awareness of your emotions is high. This is important because letting yourself be sad when you are sad and worried when you are worried, does not impede being able to access and focus on what is good in your life.

Happiness is a by-product, not the goal.

Let ease be your guide

Use ease as your guide. Not easy, but ease.

When we're struggling with a problem of any kind, it often helps to lean out to allow flow, rather than leaning in even further and pushing your way through to a solution. When we push, we constrict ourselves and lose sight of the bigger picture. It is worthwhile asking yourself if you are struggling because something is new, or because it is out of alignment with your values.

You'll remember from what you read in Chapter 3, that your comfort zone is real in the sense that your thoughts trigger emotions that signal the release of hormones into your body. So, in a sense, it is tantamount to coming up against real physical barriers. The way to work with yourself vis a vis your comfort zone is to recognise that it is safe for you to step outside of the zone.

Of course, not all discomfort is the same. It is helpful to be able to distinguish between discomfort that is worth going through because it will expand your comfort zone (that's the case when something is hard just because it is new), and discomfort that is a sign to leave the project behind or course correct (this is the case when something is hard because it is out of alignment).

The level of discernment necessary to be able to tell the difference between the two kinds of discomfort described above requires you to draw on and apply everything you have learned so far in this book. It's about knowing your strengths and your values, being aware of your thoughts (both around the specific issue in the moment, and your broader thought habits) and taking deliberate action from new and different perspectives. I believe life is meant to be easy. That's not to say that we should only do easy things. On the contrary – we can all do hard things. My point is that doing hard things doesn't necessarily make life hard. When you are the best version of yourself it will become easier for you to let ease be your guide. In the section below which is about Space, you will find a way to take this idea up another notch.

Consider whether something is hard because it is new or because it is out of alignment.

Create space

This is about slowing down to speed up.
Real transformation and progress are what take place when you allow it to happen, not when you push and struggle or clamour for it. It requires space. So lean back. Pause. Be still and quiet. Let go of expectations. Stop overthinking and second-guessing

everything. I am expressing what you need to do here in several different ways, in the hope that one of the images the words above bring to mind may resonate with you.

It is in the space where you pause and spend some time in stillness that transformation happens. The space is necessary. Sure, you might be able to create change without this kind of space. That will still be worthwhile. But if you want to truly uplevel yourself and your position, you need to create and return to this space.

What this means is that if you are not used to being by yourself, it's time for you to get used to it. This can be a challenge for people like us living in the busy world we live in, but this is important because getting in tune with yourself and feeling what you need to feel can only be done when you are on your own without interruptions. Again, this can be challenging because in this space you won't have things like your phone or your headphones, so again if you are not used to silence, it's time for you to get used to it.

Some people use this space for meditation, prayer, or quiet reflection, but it doesn't have to be used for either. Physical exercise may be part of this space, but it must not take up the whole space. There needs to be room for nothingness as well.

In this nothingness the default network of your brain is active. When that's the case solutions come to you, answers reveal themselves, and creative sparks appear. In short, this is where the magic happens. Until you allow that space into your life on a regular basis, quite literally, you will have no idea what you are missing out on, as what comes up here is not part of the five percent of your mind that you are conscious of. I want you to get used to loitering in this space, purposefully but without expectation, and get used to listening for, hearing, and little by little acting on the inklings that come up for you.

Earlier on I asked you to use the notion of ease as a guide to help you decide whether to go forward or not. When you add space to this notion you will get a sense of how to move forward. This muscle, the 'leaning back and looking for the ease'- muscle (as I call it), might be completely unused in your case to date. Don't let that worry you. Don't dismiss it, because space is what makes the difference between progress and transformation.

If you find that using this special muscle is hard, I want you to stick with it because I don't think there's a person alive for whom resistance to sitting quietly with themselves presented anything other than discomfort when they first started practising it. If you can sit in the discomfort and let it be, then little by little you will learn to trust the strength of ease and space.

My hope is that moving through this book and following its suggestions has brought you to a place where the idea of space will be a lot less challenging for you than it would have been before you started reading this book. I think of personal transformation as being a bit like shaping something out of clay. Following the suggestions covered so far in this book is like moulding the clay; moulding the best version of you, and adopting the notions of ease and space is like firing it in the kiln. I don't mean to suggest that it will harden you. Rather I'm suggesting that it will make that best version of you stronger. The fact that this section about space is positioned towards the end of the book does not mean that it is less important than the subjects you read about in the beginning. On the contrary, it might be the most important ingredient in the mix. This is because the shift you have created so far, with the new perspectives you have opened yourself up to, will take form in this new space and materialise as transformation.

Space is what makes the difference between progress and transformation.

Summary

This chapter is full of suggestions on how you can look at things differently.

Some of the suggestions in this chapter might work for any situation, while others might be best suited for certain situations. Pick and choose, and find your favourites.

When you want to achieve a different result you need to either do things differently, or do different things.

Adding a new perspective to your thoughts and your actions is an easy way to start doing things differently.

A new perspective can help in various ways. It might help you get started when you feel stuck, it might help you get past your own limiting beliefs and inhibitions, and it might remind you that different things are possible.

Remember to try a different perspective whenever you feel resistance.

It is helpful to see your progress, not just all that you still have to do.

Making decisions as if you already are the person you are aspiring to be is a way to fast-track your progress.

Get used to thinking that best-case scenarios are possible, that things are easy and that a pause can be your best way forward.

NOTES

Chapter 9

YOUR MIND CAN HOLD YOU BACK

It's worth being on guard for these things that can hold you back when you're taking action in new ways.

Old, familiar self-talk keeping you comfortable

Stay conscious of self-talk throughout your current process of change and beyond. When things are changing around you and inside you, you will meet resistance at times. This can happen because things are getting difficult, because too much around you is new, because you are getting close to the edge of your comfort zone, or for any number of other reasons. When this happens, you will feel the urge to slip back to things that are familiar and comfortable. Old thought patterns and old habits return, and they might have been full of limiting beliefs. You might even start berating yourself for thinking that change was possible. Don't worry, this is just part of the journey.

Think back to what you learnt in the section about the brain-body connection in Chapter 3, and how your familiar comfort zone in a sense has actual physical barriers around it. Remind yourself again that they are only thoughts, that it is safe for you to think new thoughts and do new things, and let your physiology catch up. Don't make the mistake of retreating into familiar territory and abandoning the progress you have made so far.

Recognise when the old self-talk is trying to keep you safe – and then realise that it is safe for you to dismiss it.

Dismissal

You have almost read this entire book about how to navigate your way through change by being the best and most authentic version of yourself. But if I know one thing for certain, it is that just reading a book won't create change. Only you can change your life. My hope is that you have taken notes and done the exercises you've come across throughout this book. That would have given you awareness and clarity. This is important because without awareness, deliberate action is not possible. And without clarity, the process of change becomes unnecessarily difficult and lengthy.

The suggestions in Chapter 8 related to *how* to do things, not *what* to do. It is up to you to apply them to the action that is required in relation to the change you are wanting to achieve. One thing is for certain, however, and that is that action is required. We can sit here and theorise all we want, but if you are after a different result in your life you will need to *do* things differently.

One thing that you can't afford to do when you are trying to do things differently is dismiss advice before you give it a try. Remember that when the aim is a different perspective, the advice might well sound new or strange or different to you. That's the whole point. Tools are only helpful if you use them.

Not even something as concrete as a hammer can be of help if it just stays in the toolbox. You need to pick it up and use it for it to have any impact.

Don't dismiss tools before you try them.

Perfectionism

Let me guess; either you are truly surprised to find perfectionism in a chapter about things to look out for, or you are nodding your head in recognition of something you are all too familiar with.

If you are one of the people who are surprised to find perfectionism here, chances are that you see it as a virtue. You take pride in declaring yourself a perfectionist because you feel it conveys the very high standards that you live by and strive for. You're probably one of those people who replies to the question (that comes up in almost every job interview) about what your weaknesses are by saying, "I am a bit of a perfectionist, I suppose," with a little laugh to signify that you don't see it as a weakness at all, and you just want to appear humble by avoiding saying that you don't have any weaknesses.

Here is the truth: Perfectionism is an excuse people use for not taking action. Perfectionism is the safety blanket of intelligent, educated and capable people like yourself. The problem with perfectionism is that it makes you stay stuck forever, as there will always be something that you can make just a little bit better, and always something more to learn before you are fully done.

You need to be brave enough to see perfectionism as the weakness and opportunity-limiting excuse that it is. You might feel uncomfortable about this. You may think you have to lower your standards if you are going to let go of work before it is perfect. But the truth is that no one benefits from work that never gets finished, not even you. What does it matter if it could be one percent better if no one gets to see it?

My advice to you is to let go of perfectionism as an excuse, take the uncomfortable action, and do it anyway. Whatever it is you are procrastinating about by exercising perfectionism, know that your first go at something new is like a trial run anyway. It's best to see how it goes and correct where needed, otherwise perfectionism will stop you from fulfilling your full potential.

Don't hide behind perfectionism. It often results in eternal procrastination. Besides, the process of change is, by its very nature, rather imperfect.

Take small steps to get yourself out of perfectionism and procrastination. Small steps will move you forward and give you momentum even when you feel like you don't have much to give. The other great thing about small steps is that they hide imperfection rather well.

Don't let perfectionism become procrastination.

Summary

In the midst of change, your brain will want to find reasons to go back to old familiar ways. Beware of it so that you stay in control and keep moving forward.

Don't dismiss new ideas before you try them.

Perfectionism is nothing other than an excuse if it stops you from ever getting ready.

NOTES

NOTES

Chapter 10

COAX YOURSELF FORWARD

The goal is to have enough positive energy to keep moving forward into new and unknown territory. The truth is that sometimes you won't. Change can be tough, as well as tiring for the brain and therefore for the body. If you are putting the strategies and techniques suggested in this book to good use, you will be doing a lot of conscious thinking, rather than letting your thoughts go on autopilot like you have been used to. A new conscious soundtrack that you got from Chapter 3, new perspectives from Chapter 8, and staying away from the pitfalls in Chapter 9, all take energy, and sometimes you might feel that you need a break.

Here are some thoughts you can use to keep yourself moving forward even then.

Maybe

When everything seems big, new and insurmountable, generalisations and exaggerations are close at hand. Your mind closes over and tells you there is no way you will be able to do everything that is required. That's when you can benefit from injecting a *Maybe* into your thinking.

Maybe can open a crack just big enough to let the smallest ray of light in. And possibly that's all it takes to get you moving.

When the voice in your head says, "I will never finish all this by the weekend," tell it "Maybe I can get most of it done." When your mind tells you "I will never get the pay rise I want" tell it "Maybe I can at least start a conversation about it with my boss." *Maybe* can help open the door to a closed mind the tiniest crack so that you can at least start thinking that one day there might be a way.

The beauty is that a door that is cracked open is so much easier to open than a door that is firmly shut.

'Maybe' can open a closed mind.

Yet

Another helpful word is *yet*. Make a habit of finishing a sentence where you voice any shortcomings, inadequacy or lack with this little word. Sentences like – "I don't know how to do that – yet," and "I have never held a position of leadership – yet" take advantage of a small and uncomplicated trick that unapologetically throws aside any sense of limitations and gets you straight into the territory of a growth mindset.

'Yet' is ripe with possibilities.

Add familiarity where you can

When most things are new and unfamiliar around you, that in itself can increase your level of stress and uncertainty. You can feel like you no longer have an anchor point. It is also rather exhausting, as your brain has very few automated behaviours to rely on. In these cases, try to add familiarity where you can. Stick to a daily routine: get up at the same time each morning and set up a healthy set of habits that give you energy and motivation to get through the day. Put the things you need to do in your calendar as that can help to give you a sense of purpose and help you to track what you do.

You might be someone who normally doesn't like the monotony of routines, and instead try to find different ways of doing things, and different routes to get where you are going so that you won't get bored. In times when it feels like everything is up in the air you might find it helpful to do the opposite, and add familiarity by sticking to the usual way. Routines and familiarity give your mind some rest when it has to deal with a lot of change.

> **Give your mind a rest by adding familiar routines.**

That is what I had to do myself as I was writing this book. I have already shared that I followed my own advice to act as my new identity, so to centre myself and focus I would ask myself, "What would a writer do?" This served me well several times and got me moving forward.

However, as so much in my daily life felt new and unfamiliar, I sometimes found myself stuck and exhausted. I then needed to use another piece of advice and add some familiarity. I reminded myself that I had always been a person who got things done, and I needed to draw on the strengths of that person. For that to happen, I needed to look back, not forward, and I asked myself, "What would a pilot do?"

That question brought me back to structures and processes that were familiar to me. Even as I was taking action, I was able to rest in that familiarity. As a pilot, I told myself I would systematically do what I needed to do until it was all done.

So it was that I became an author by channelling my inner pilot.

Rephrase words with baggage

Commitment is a word you often hear when people are talking about achieving just about anything worthwhile. Personally, I've struggled with that word over time. It sounds like a punch in the stomach to me. Yet I have been committed to lots of things during my life and achieved them. My trouble is not with committing to doing what I need to do, but with the very word itself. I have had to find other ways to achieve the same results without using the word 'commitment'. The words 'effortless commitment' sounded playful and light enough for me to get on board. Vision is something else that I find easy to agree with and work towards. Drive is also something I can easily find.

The point here is that there are times when semantics matter a lot, so don't let someone else's phraseology stop you from moving forward.

Don't let someone else's phraseology stop you from moving forward.

If you stumble on advice good enough that you can see it might take you in the right direction but there is still something in you that opposes it, take a moment and consider what it is. Find your own words for the same situation, words that are helpful in terms of supporting you to take the next right step. I invite you to do so with what you read in this book. However, a caveat is required here. This particular section is all about different perspectives and doing things differently. I really do want you to try these suggestions out. As you know, you can't keep doing the same thing the same way and expect different results. This is where I want to invite you to shift your thinking. So, if you need to change a word to get your reluctant self on board, do so, but please keep hold of the different perspective.

People don't care – and that's a good thing!

People care about you and your apparent flaws much less than you think. The fact of the matter is that all eyes are not on you. People don't have an opinion about you and the things that you do.

I am saying these things here not to shoot you down, but to set you free. I hope you can see that since you are not the centre of everyone's attention, you are quite free to do, try, learn, and grow as required.

When you realise that everyone is busy living their own life it leaves you room to feel ok about being imperfect. Giving yourself room to be imperfect is the quickest way to become the very best version of yourself that you can be.

While we are talking about people's opinions, I want you to realise that when they do have them, those opinions say more about them, than about you. Opinions show the other person's filters and fears, and if anything, they are only vaguely relevant to you.

Be liberated by the fact that people don't care as much about you as you think.

Self-compassion

Give yourself compassion. Acknowledge all that you have done and let that, at least for a moment, be more important than everything you still need to do. Celebrate the new things that you have accomplished and allow yourself to feel good about them.

Treat yourself as well as you would treat a good friend. I am certain that you have given compassionate advice to a friend many times, telling her to not be too hard on herself, and to give herself credit for what she has achieved, rather than beat herself up for what she hasn't.

Please do the same for yourself. When things get hard, when you want to quit or you are ready to berate yourself for whatever reason, stop and think, "What would I tell my friend in this situation?"

Treat yourself as well as you would treat a good friend.

Gratitude

The act of making gratitude a habit comes with the by-product of making us more resilient. We don't have to be grateful for the hardship that we are going through. Simply being able to find gratitude for something, anything, is beneficial. It contributes positively to the filter through which we see the world, and when we start looking for things to be grateful for, we will see more and more of them. This adds a sense of possibility and abundance as we start seeing what we have, rather than what we are missing.

One easy way to do this is to keep a gratitude journal, and at the end of each day consider three things you are grateful for. When you do this, don't be tempted to think that it needs to be a case of checks and balances. You can allow yourself to remember only the good things without feeling dishonest. Below is an example that illustrates this.

Let's say you've had a really bad day. Your alarm didn't go off, so you overslept and your whole morning felt rushed and stressful. Then your bus didn't turn up on time and you were further delayed. Of course, it was a rainy morning, and when you walked the last block to your office you got drenched. The meeting you had didn't go well, and you lost a valuable client. You can't wait for your workday to be over so you can go home. When it's finally over, you walk to the bus again in the rain, and all of a sudden you catch a whiff of a wonderful smell as someone opens a shop door. You look up to see a beautiful florist shop. Inside it looks bright and warm amongst all the flowers and the smiling people in there. It puts a smile on your face for a second too, before you get splashed by a car as it drives past through a big puddle that drenches you. By the time you get home you are soaked through, exhausted and in a bad mood after all the challenges you encountered during the day.

Before you turn out the light for the day you think back over your day to pick one moment to remember the day for. There is nothing wrong with picking the 10 seconds you smelled the flowers and looked into that warm cosy florist shop as your memory for the day. It doesn't need to represent the day. You are not hiding from the truth or lying to yourself by not bringing the less positive events of the day to mind. What you are doing is setting yourself up to feel good and be inclined to notice more good things as you move about in your life. This is key because when you feel good you can perform better, find better solutions, make better decisions, bounce back quicker … The benefits are almost endless, and the risks are none.

Be grateful for good things in your life, and you will set yourself up to notice more good things to be grateful for.

Summary

Going through change is stressful and tiring. Allow yourself to rest in familiar routines and gentle thoughts while still not slipping back to old habits or inaction.

'Maybe' and 'yet' are words that can help coax you forward even when things feel rather impossible.

Show yourself the same kindness and understanding that you would show a friend.

Practising gratitude will show you more things to be grateful for.

A whole day can be summarised by the best minute of it.

NOTES

NOTES

CONCLUSION

You have come to the end of this book, but you are only at the beginning of the transformation that is possible for you.

I hope that you have already seen shifts in your thoughts, and that you can see yourself and your potential in a new light. You can likely see that you don't need to reach for the next thing 'out there' but you can access it from the inside instead. So often we are our own worst enemies, thinking limiting and demeaning thoughts. The good news is that while you are the problem, you are also the solution. What you need is a different thought and a different perspective. The best news of all is that changing your perspective is not as hard as you may have thought before reading this book. Creating a new pathway and a new future is an opportunity that is always available to you, especially if you make your thoughts your ally and choose ones that are helpful to you in each moment.

It's in our nature to want to achieve great things. Somehow we know on some level that great things are possible. And we are so right! Our brain works best when it is given a challenge, something just outside its current capacity to strive for. That's when it finds new solutions and new ways to do things. This is how we optimise our potential and get to really discover our strengths.

Being continually motivated to learn and to grow will put you on a path that will inevitably lead to success, whatever that means to you.

It is not hard, but it might not be how you are used to working.

Like most people, I suspect you are becoming more used to dealing with change. Heaven knows we have all had to navigate so much change and uncertainty in the last few years. When there is no other alternative, we are forced to uplevel our flexibility around our capacities. Hopefully, you too can coax yourself forward with the ideas in this book, just like I did, and find a way to change with less struggle and more ease. It is my wish that the example of my gentle way to move mountains will be of some help to you in being able to play with your mind until it thinks that difficult things are easy. You only need a moment, enough to take some small action, and then the momentum will move you forward.

It's time for me to sign off now. I want to leave you with the challenge to not just put this book down and do nothing about your goals and aspirations. I trust you to remember that even the greatest achievements are made up of small steps, and what you need to do is break the task down until each piece is small enough to feel achievable. If you are in any doubt, I want you to pick the book up again and follow one of the suggestions in it. It doesn't matter which one because any shift in your energy is likely to get you motivated again.

Each point in this book is enough to create a significant shift. At the same time, each point also has more depth than what I have been able to fit into this book, and holds more potential for those interested in really up levelling themselves. If that is you, I invite you to connect with me so I can provide more value and assistance to you over time.

END NOTE

It is the evening of your 70th birthday. Friends and family stopped by during the day to congratulate you and celebrate with you. Someone even asked you, "What is it like to be such a successful …?" This got you thinking about how it started. How decades ago, you realised that it wasn't so much in the doing, but in the being.

You learned the importance of knowing and working from your strengths, and you remember the shift this created in you at the time.

You learned to use your values as your compass, and ever since you have made your choices and decisions effortlessly, without being riddled with conflict and guilt.

You became aware of your thoughts, and since then have always had a helpful soundtrack in your head.

You embraced all that you were, and that way you became the best version of yourself.

Instead of striving to do 'that thing,' you started striving to be 'that person.'

All the fantastic things you went on to do were happy by-products.

My hope is that this book has helped in setting you on that trajectory of *Growing Forward*.

www.ingramcontent.com/pod-product-compliance
Lightning Source LLC
Chambersburg PA
CBHW020322010526
44107CB00054B/1947